THEATRE SYMPOSIUM
A JOURNAL OF THE SOUTHEASTERN THEATRE CONFERENCE

KT-368-112

Volume I *Contents* **1993**

Introduction   5

PART I

The Uses of Music in *Commedia* Performance   7
  Thomas F. Heck

Creative Contrarities: The *Commedia* Heritage   13
  John Swan

A Semiotic Perspective on the *Commedia dell'Arte*   20
  Michael L. Quinn

Commedia dell'Arte and the Spanish Golden Age Theatre   28
  Nancy L. D'Antuono

The Influence of *Commedia dell'Arte Scenari* on the
  Modern Stage   36
  James Fisher

Symposium Discussion   41

PART II

A Renaissance Anomaly: A *Commedia dell'Arte* Troupe
  in Residence at the Court Theatre at Sabbioneta   57
  Stanley V. Longman

A Semiotic Interpretation of the *Lazzi* of the
  Commedia dell'Arte   66
  Anna L. Moro

Watteau's *Commedia* and the Theatricality of
  French Painting   77
  Michael L. Quinn

Ebullience and Edification from a Modern *Commediante*   94
Thomas A. Pallen

Commedia at Coney Island   104
Christopher C. Newton

Polichinelle in Paris: Puppetry and the
Commedia dell'Arte   116
Jane McMahan

Controversy, Cops, and *Commedia:* Staging the
Throwaway Farce of Fo's *Accidental Death of
an Anarchist*   127
James Fisher

Commedia in the Classroom: *Commedia dell'Arte*
Performance, Shakespearean Pedagogy, and
Popular Culture   135
Georgeann Murphy

Contributors   143

THEATRE SYMPOSIUM
A JOURNAL OF THE SOUTHEASTERN THEATRE CONFERENCE

Commedia dell'Arte Performance

Contexts and Contents

Published by the

Southeastern Theatre Conference and

The University of Alabama Press

THEATRE SYMPOSIUM is published annually by the Southeastern Theatre Conference, Inc. (SETC), and by The University of Alabama Press. SETC non-student members receive the journal as a part of their membership under rules determined by SETC. For information on membership, write to SETC, P.O. Box 9868, Greensboro, NC 27429–0868. *All other inquiries* regarding subscriptions, circulation, purchase of individual copies, and requests to reprint material should be addressed to The University of Alabama Press, P.O. Box 870380, Tuscaloosa, AL 35487–0380.

THEATRE SYMPOSIUM publishes works of scholarship resulting from a single-topic meeting held on a southeastern university campus each spring. A call for papers to be presented at that meeting is widely publicized each autumn for the following spring. Thus, unsolicited manuscripts sent directly to the editor are not encouraged. Information about the next symposium is available from Philip G. Hill, Department of Drama, Furman University, Greenville, SC 29613.

Introduction

TWENTY-SIX SCHOLARS gathered on the campus of The University of Alabama on April 10–12, 1992, to examine some of the latest scholarship relating to *commedia dell'arte*. Under the leadership of Symposium Director Paul Castagno, a panel of five *commedia* experts responded to a packet of primary material that had been prepared for them, and eighteen other papers focusing on various aspects of *commedia* were also read. Through a refereeing process, the Editorial Board selected seven of these eighteen papers to be published in Part II of this volume.

Part I was assembled by recording, transcribing, and editing the contributions of the five symposium participants. Each of them made a short presentation reacting to the primary material, and there was then a general discussion among them led by Paul Castagno; the five panelists were Nancy D'Antuono (St. Mary's College, IN), James Fisher (Wabash College, IN), Thomas F. Heck (Ohio State University), Michael L. Quinn (University of Washington), and John Swan (Bennington College, VT).

Since the primary materials to which the panel responded are readily available in most libraries, they have not been reprinted here. *The Enchanted Wood* and *The Madness of Isabella* are *commedia dell'arte* scenarios from Flaminio Scala's *Il Teatro delle favole rappresentative* and are available in a translation by Henry F. Salerno entitled *Scenarios of the Commedia dell'Arte* (New York: New York University Press, 1967), pages 378–384 and 282–291 respectively. *Innocence Restored* is a scenario from Locatelli translated by K. M. Lea in her *Italian Popular Comedy* (Oxford: Clarendon Press, 1934), volume 2, pages 573–579. Other documents were selected from Kenneth and Laura Richards' *The Commedia dell'Arte: A Documen-*

tary History (Oxford: Shakespeare Head Press, 1990), and appropriate page references appear throughout the ensuing discussion.

The editor wishes to express deep appreciation to The University of Alabama, and to the scholars, many of whom traveled great distances to participate in the symposium and its related events. The excellence of the material in this volume is attributable to all of these participants.

Part I

The Uses of Music in

Commedia Performance

Thomas F. Heck

THERE ARE INTRIGUING parallels between improvised music such as jazz and improvised theatre such as the *commedia dell'arte*. Both genres require that the performers have a flawless sense of rhythm and style; they must make their entrances on cue and play their parts in character. Most saliently, both art forms stand or fall on the performer's ability to embroider upon some kind of skeletal structure, whether it be a plot outline in a scenario collection or a one-line score with chord symbols in a "fake book."

The notion of "embroidering" brings to mind a common misconception regarding the meaning of a term frequently encountered in *commedia* literature, namely the *canovaccio* (Italian) or *canevas* (French). The terms refer to the plot outline or *scenario* that undergirds a *commedia* performance. Well-meaning etymologists in the theatre history community, perhaps having at their disposal a French or Italian pocket dictionary that offers "canvas" as a functional English equivalent, have suggested that the term's theatrical usage derives from the alleged performance practice of taking a scenario and pinning it to the "canvas," that is, the backdrop of the open-air platform stage sometimes used by itinerant *commedia* troupes. The actors—as this just-so story goes—would glance at these sheets just before making their entrances, using them as a kind of *aide-mémoire*. This may sound plausible, but when I looked up *canovaccio* in several native Italian encyclopedias and Italian etymological dictionaries, it became clear that for centuries it has had a special significance in embroidery. It means a piece of loosely woven cloth on which a line or pattern has been traced, upon which one embroiders, adding color and texture in the process. The French cognate is *canevas*. We need no longer speculate, therefore, on the presumed practice of pinning scenarios on canvas backdrops. Rather, we can now be satisfied with a perfectly plausible and relevant etymology for *canovaccio,* taken directly from the art of embroidery, which fits the nature of *commedia* performance much better than the canvas-backdrop theory.

In what way does all this relate to music? Let me count the ways: (A) The whole phenomenon of improvised figured bass, a numeric (actually intervallic) notation for keyboard players commonly encountered in scores dating roughly from 1600 to 1760, is nothing if not a case of musicians embroidering on a line, in this instance a carefully constructed bass line. The resulting sound and texture noticeably enhanced the quality and tone color of the (otherwise monochromatic) bass line. (B) During the sixteenth and early seventeenth centuries dozens of books of guitar tablature were produced, in which not even a musical staff is discernible. Instead, one finds simply a single line (a time-line, as it were) with chord letters and tick marks showing when and how to strum: up or down.

One of the earliest notated dances for the guitar was, in fact, the *folia.* It required that the peformers improvise a set of variations over a chord pattern. The harmonic progression, in modern chord notation, might look and sound rather familiar:

d	–	A	–	d	–	C
F	–	C	–	d	–	A
d	–	A	–	d	–	C
F	–	C	–	d/A	–	d

Another such chord pattern of the sixteenth century was the *ciaccona,* forerunner of the highly stylized baroque *chaconne* of some two hundred years later. Margherita Costa's play *Li Buffoni* (Florence, 1641), recently published in *Commedie dell'arte,* the anthology of plays by professional Italian actors (Ferrone 1986, 233–357), includes a text for a "Canzonetta da cantarsi e ballarsi in ciaccona," a canzonetta to sing and dance to the strains of the *ciaccona.* It is printed at the back of the play, evidently being intended as something special for the third act, subject to the availability of a suitable singer and guitarist. One would like to suppose that any reasonably trained actor or actress of the era knew how the *ciaccona* went—it was such a commonplace—and could probably sing endless vocal "riffs" or take-offs on the tune or chords. Iconographic sources confirm repeatedly that guitars and lutes (the former more frequently) were used both on and off stage to accompany songs and dances in *commedia* performance.

Those who have worked with *commedia* scenarios know that many call explicitly for some kind of music somewhere in the play. Often the specific instruments needed are listed in the *roba*, that is, the "stuff" or props that we find often at the beginning of each play. Even if instruments are not mentioned, it seems quite clear that there are numerous places where musical accompaniment is called for. For example, in *The Enchanted Wood* we see that "Corinto . . . enters playing his pipe and singing of his love for the nymph he saw hidden in a fountain." A musicologist would probably speculate that he is singing a *canzonetta* of the sixteenth or early seventeenth century, most likely accompanied by any available chordal instrument (probably a guitar); refrains would perhaps have been played on the flute (i.e., pipe). There are places in this scenario that are less obvious as to their potential for musical embellishment. In the middle of Act 1, Timbri "shows them the grotto of the magician, asking one of them to fetch from within a veil of silk" and so on, and at that moment flames of fire shoot out from the grotto. There are other occurrences where the grotto is mentioned specifically with reference to noise. In my study of instruments depicted in iconographical sources that would have been at the disposal of the *comici dell'arte*, I came to realize that about twenty to thirty percent of the instruments used were of the type known as idiophones: percussion instruments, noise-makers, rattles, xylophones, castanets, things of this sort. The *comici* had, within their musical ménage, what was necessary to make weird and exotic noises.

In another scenario, *Innocence Restored,* you will notice that the theme of the Turk is somewhat prominent. There is a Turk in the production, Rais the Turk, and you are probably familiar with the Shakespeare play, *Cymbeline,* which may be derived from this source. I think the exotic land would be Rome; there are many quick scene changes between England and Rome in Shakespeare's play. In both cases, the musical implication is, to me, fairly clear. That is to say, before the Turk enters onstage, one might use the oriental-sounding instruments. I am thinking of a *colascione* for instance, which is a long-wired lute that is evident in the Callot engravings. It makes an oriental, twanging sound. It is easy to add atmosphere with the right kind of music, and there were various exotic instruments available to the *comici dell'arte* and no doubt used for these exotic scenes.

An oracle to the Duke comes in at the beginning of Act 1 of *Innocence Restored,* and that is the only example of written-out text in the whole scenario. I suggest that it most probably would have been intoned in some way. There is another place, at the beginning of Act 2, where the Duke returns to the oracle, and you could have comparable music to introduce that scene, even if the oracle does not give the answer that is requested. It is still dramatically appropriate to "refer back" with a musical device.

In another scenario, *The Madness of Isabella,* there is a scene in which Isabella, in a frenzy, "began to speak in French, and also to sing songs in the French manner which gave such pleasure to the most serene bride, the Duke's wife, that no one could have been more delighted," and then she went on to imitate the other actors (Richards and Richards 1990, 74–75). Here is a firsthand account of Isabella singing in French in 1589.

What might she have been singing? Here's where you need to knock on the door of your friendly musicologist. I came up with two examples of something Isabella might well have sung. The first is a French *air de cour,* which is usually for voice and lute, sometimes for voice and harpsichord. The composer is Jacques Mauduit, who was born in 1557, and the title is "Eau Vive Source d'Amour." The *air de cour* involves a declamatory style with special emphasis on the rhythm of the words. It seems to have been a musical response to Jean Antione Baïf and his circle of French poets who were so concerned with declamation just as French was really becoming an art language. (MUSIC: see album, *Airs from the Courts of Henri IV and Louis XIII,* Turnabout TVS 34316, side 1, band 2.) You cannot beat time to this song because the rhythm is taken from the text itself. It is perhaps liberating for people in theatre to know that you do not have to sound like you are doing a dance or "something a drummer can drum" to make an authentic musical interpretation of a section of text in a given theatrical situation.

Nevertheless, there is another style of song that does have the musical rhythm dominate, that is to say, it presents a regular, steady beat. We call these "dance airs" or "dance tunes" because of their rhythmic regularity. An example from the same period would be "Beaux yeux," or Beautiful Eyes. This is the French equivalent of the *canzonetta,* which is found in many Italian sources; the present one is by Jean Baptiste Bésard, who was born in 1567. (MUSIC: see album *Ancient Airs and Dances,* Paul O'Dette and Roger Covey, Hyperion CDA 66228, track 18.) Can you imagine Isabella singing a lilting little dance air like this one on stage as part of her *pazzia* scene? I can. I have no problem at all. She could perform with a guitar accompaniment, she could clap her hands and do it, or she could spin around and sing—there are many possibilities. Of course, there were a thousand *airs de cour* published between 1600 and

1650, for it was an enormously popular genre—the French equivalent of the English lute song.

Another interesting reference in *The Madness of Isabella* is found in Act 3 of the Scala scenario. Isabella has a series of crazy episodes when she returns. "They stop to listen, and she begins to speak: 'I remember the year I could not remember that a harpsichord sat beside a Spanish Pavane dancing with a gagliarda of Santin of Parma, after which the lasagne, the macaroni, and the polenta'" so on and so forth. Nonsense of course. Yes? But if you take the trouble to look up the reference, you realize that it is even more nonsense than what appears on the surface, because a Spanish pavane is a stately dance in double meter and a *gagliarda* is a dance in triple meter; the two just do not go together. As a footnote, the "Santin of Parma" is a corrupt reference to Santino Garci da Parma who was a sixteenth-century lutanist. On the album called *Ancient Airs and Dances,* there is an actual *gagliarda* by Garci da Parma called "La Cesarina." (MUSIC: "Spanish Pavan" by Alfonso Ferrabosso from the album *"English Lute Duets,"* Paul O'Dette and Jacob Lindburg, BLS, LP-267). The reason I mention these examples is not to say that they were interpolated into the mad scene, but they could have been. We know of their existence because we have the specific references, but in any event it is interesting to realize what the passage means in musical terms; upon hearing the music, we grasp the incongruity all the more.

Richards and Richards (1990, 149) contains a description of the set pieces that could be drawn on by professional actors. In one, "Two Soliloquies of a Lover," are a couple of little sections in verse. One of them is "That in amorous calm in that beautiful breast, / Thoughts, heart and soul will find joyful rest" (1990, 182). Usually when I scan a theatrical text looking for musical implications, my eye will gravitate to the shorter-lined poetry within a longer section of prose. One develops this skill when working with opera librettos, because in opera librettos typically the arias have the briefest text of all, yet the most musical.

Other interesting uses of music in *commedia* performance are found in three plays from volume 2 of Ferrone (1986). One is seen in Margherita Costa's play, *Li Buffoni,* and is entitled "Canzonnetta da cantarsi a tre voci principio della commedia innanzi il prologo" (1986, 243). It is a three-voice *canzonetta* and makes me think of one of the famous Fossard engravings that shows three men, the Pantalone and two *zanni,* serenading a woman in a tower. Three-voice *canzonette* were very common at this time. Other scenes demonstrate singing entrances and singing exits (Ferrone 1986, 49, 71, 73–75, 246, 268–69, 333, 340–41) and include an episode in which a person goes from dancing to singing and someone actually hands him a guitar and says, "Here, strum away" (1986, 305). In summary, I find the evidence of incidental music in *commedia dell'arte* quite overwhelming, whether in iconographical sources or in the extant written record.

Works Cited

Ferrone, Siro, ed. *Commedie dell'Arte*. 2 vols. Milan: Mursia, 1985 and 1986.
Richards, Kenneth, and Laura Richards. *The* Commedia dell'Arte: *A Documentary History*. Oxford: Shakespeare Head Press, 1990.

Creative Contrarities

The *Commedia* Heritage

John Swan

THE COMMEDIA DELL'ARTE has always been a paradoxical art, at least since the time it became a self-conscious form of theatre. After all, its essential structures have their built-in contradictions: improvisatory freedom rooted in carefully rehearsed mastery; plots of exfoliating complexity based on the simplest of routines; extremes of emotion and expressive license embodied in characters of clear definition and proportion, who never, for long, lose their symmetrical relationships among one another. Isabella's madness, like Ophelia's, like that of Lucia di Lammermoor, is deranged suffering, but it is also a star turn—not merely for the woman who gets the part, but for the character—which blossoms into a richly theatricalized identity. The shifts between sanity and madness, forgetting and remembering, that take place within *The Enchanted Wood* may confuse and dismay for a time, but they serve in the end to emphasize, not blur, the distinction between characters and their personalities, preoccupations, and status. It is thus also on Prospero's island and in Oberon's enchanted forest.

These paradoxes of order and disorder, proportion and extravagance, are not confined to the world of *commedia*, to be sure; versions thereof hover in the background of all theatre. But *commedia* flaunts its theatricality, celebrates its freedom to drag chaos out of order and then shove it back into the night; it relies on the visibility and stability of its stereotypes, both in character and in action, in order to embellish, destroy, and recreate them. The tensions of contradiction are more vivid, more clearly an essential source of dramatic energy. It is natural, therefore, that there is much paradox in the influence of *commedia* upon modernist and contemporary theatre.

One such paradox, or cluster of paradoxes, can be seen in the uses to which *commedia* is put by those who see in it the power to take drama beyond its accepted boundaries and make of it the engine of social change. This is certainly what the modernists saw in their own way when the world was bright with promise at the beginning of the century— remember Alexander Blok's letter to Meyerhold at the time of the epochal Fairground Booth of 1906: "Any farce, mine included, strives to be a battering ram, to break through the lifeless . . . In the embraces of a fool and a farce the old world will wax beautiful and grow young, and its eyes will become clear, fathomless" (Rudnitsky 1981, 105). Several revolutions have come, triumphed, and been betrayed since then, and the nature of the battering ram has changed. There is a considerable distance between the "commedic" revolution of a group of reformed Symbolists and the social revolution attempted by today's leading theatrical activists, especially those with roots in real folk theatre.

When Ron Jenkins asked Dario Fo the reason for his particular choice of character in *Hellequin, Arlekin, Arlechino,* the reply showed that an awareness of paradox was central to that choice: "I have been playing Harlequin my entire career. My characters have always been in this key. Harlequin is a character who destroys all conventions. His personality and sense of morals are based on paradox. He comes out of nothing and can transform himself into anything" (Jenkins 1986, 11). Fo's Harlequin is a cheerfully obscene clown who can draw upon elemental forces when he expresses the rage and the hunger that come from deprivation, poverty, and injustice—in Fo's words, "This was Harlequin's style before he was refined by playwrights like Goldoni. . . . This is what Harlequin was like before he was castrated" (quoted in Jenkins 1986, 11). He is present, for example, in the opening scene of *Mistero Buffo,* in which the desperately hungry peasant, driven to self-cannibalization, literally demonstrates Fo's version of Harlequin's paradox: "The instincts for self-preservation and self-annihilation cancel each other out as he gobbles up his body parts until there is nothing left but a mouth vainly trying to devour itself out of existence" (Jenkins 1986, 16). But Fo has more in mind than appetite in his sense of Harlequin's power, as is clear in his most famous version of the character, the "histriomaniac" in *Accidental Death of an Anarchist.* Here the character's intelligence and scathing wit set off his powers of disguise and transformation—the ability, again, to come out of nowhere and become anything.

This kind of paradox is formal and intrinsic to both Fo's theatre and the kind of *commedia* out of which he consciously evolves. Arlecchino and

Pedrolino exist within a context that gives them not only dramatic identity but also the freedom to transform, distort, and improvise upon that identity, according to the needs of plot and the personality and skills of the player. Indeed, the dramatic structure absolutely requires this display of individuality. Without that freedom and that skill, the multiple enchantments and character shifts in Flaminio Scala's *The Enchanted Wood* would never have life. And just as the old *scenari* lie flat on the page without this creative dimension, so too does the dizzying array of identities in *Mistero Buffo* depend utterly on the mimetic and dramatic powers of the protagonist.

There is another kind of paradox in the relationship of the contemporary *commedia* revolutionary to the original that is external to the formal context, but nonetheless telling. That is, there is a profound conservatism at the heart of their radicalism. This relationship is essentially what Fo means in his commitment to Harlequin "before he was castrated." Incidentally, this radical perspective—in the sense of a strong awareness of roots—lies behind Ron Jenkins's use of the same image in another setting: "If Arlecchino were castrated, dressed up in a business suit, and tied to a chair in a Burbank, California television studio, he would end up looking a lot like Johnny Carson" (Jenkins 1990, 48). Fo's scorn is perhaps more sweeping, at least in its embrace of all that happened to the *commedia* at the hands of Goldoni and his successors, but the shared sense of the loss of Harlequin's virile, primitive force is clear enough.

Joseph Farrell expressed this aspect of the Fo aesthetic paradox in terms of his social commitment: "If on the one hand Fo is customarily seen, and indeed goes out of his way to present himself, as the subversive, the iconoclastic revolutionary, the admirer of Marx and Mao, . . . at the same time his theatrical style is not based on any avant-garde, but on the approaches and techniques practiced by performers of centuries past. It is not too much to present Dario Fo as a political progressive but a theatrical conservative, and his plays and performances as a unique combination of the two" (1989, 315). True enough, but to understand this paradox properly it is important to remember that the aesthetic conservatism is itself a political commitment, determined largely by strategic choices.

Franca Rame explained this connection from a uniquely qualified position, having grown up in a family that made its living doing improvisatory people's theatre from literally the time of original *commedia dell'arte* until the competition from television and radio made such a living too difficult in the mid 1950s: "It's the usual story. The great kings, the potentates who understand such things, have always paid fools to recite before a public of highly educated courtiers, their rigmaroles of satirical humours and even of irreverent allusions to their masters' power and injustices. The courtiers could exclaim in amazement: 'What a democratic king! He has the moral strength to laugh at himself!'" The same thing happens with the irreverence of Johnny Carson or Jay Leno; name your own prosperously satiric comedian. Rame continues: "But we well know that, if the fools had been impudent enough to leave the court and sing the same satires in the town squares, before the peasants, the workers and the exploited, the king and his sycophants would pay them back in different currency. . . . No longer could we act as intellectuals, sitting comfortably within and above our own privileges, deigning in our goodness to deal with the predicament of the exploited. We had to place ourselves entirely at the service of the exploited, become their minstrels" (1978).

Rame has expressed perhaps the greatest aesthetic/social tension within the *commedia* heritage. If this theatre was born illegitimate, in the streets and villages with the *saltimbanques* and the *giullari*—and in the conviction of Fo and the experience of Rame, it certainly was—then the form taken up and revived and reformed by intellectuals and self-conscious artists must return to the streets to regain its true legitimacy. Make no mistake, Fo and Rame are self-conscious creators of a theatrical aesthetic, for all their roots in and commitment to an art not captive to the reigning powers in society.

Explaining this tension from another angle may demonstrate that it is not a glib irony, but very much of the essence creatively. Peter Schumann, another great practitioner of social and spiritual revolution through theatre and ritual performance, presents a different style and "look" from that of Fo, but they too are conditioned by a profound awareness of the *commedia* and allied folk traditions—an awareness that, like Franca Rame's, is rooted in his own growing up. His essay, "The Radicality of the Puppet Theatre," expresses the Bread and Puppet group's creative philosophy, with the same scorn of establishment art expressed by Fo and Rame, and a parallel commitment to the values of revolution:

> The puppeteers' traditional exemption from seriousness . . . and their asocial status acted also as their saving grace, as a negative privilege that allowed their art to grow. . . . The modern German puppet-interpreters have come up with a grand solution to the social-status-problem of puppetry, rebaptizing it "Figurentheater," so that nobody will find them guilty of complicity with Kasper, Punch, or Petroushka. . . . Despite the general tendency of our cultural effects to be subservient to the power of the market, to money-making and to the associated steeping of our souls into as much nonsense as possible, despite the fact that puppet theatre exists mostly in the feeble manner of an art obedient to the demands of the entertainment

business, puppet theatre also exists as a radically new and daring art form: new, not in the sense of unheard-of-newness, but in the sense of an un-covered truth. . . . Radical in the sense of not only turning away from estab-lished concepts, it also succeeded in a widening of the heart that allowed for greater inclusion of more modern and ancient art into the ancient art of puppetry. (1991)

Peter Schumann and his colleagues, no less than Fo and Rame, have built their art against a background of sophisticated awareness of the traditions that evolved out of the *commedia dell'arte,* from clowning and pantomime to Brechtian epic theatre. The Bread and Puppet Theatre is different from that of Fo, obviously, even in such basic dramatic assump-tions as the role of the professional, even virtuoso actor, so central to Fo and eschewed by Schumann. The Domestic Resurrection Circus would accommodate Fo's Harlequin very uneasily, if at all. But like Fo, Schu-mann marshals a vast theatrical arsenal in order to create an emotionally direct and compelling dramatic art. And like Fo's theatre, the dramas and rituals of Bread and Puppet are self-conscious, self-reflective expressions of theatricality. They are no more simple amateur pageants than Fo is a simple *giullare.*

It is this paradox that these contemporary descendants of *commedia* have brought to their art from the thing itself. Indeed, it was no less essential to the modernists who preceded them. The revolt against real-istic theatre seized as a central weapon the ability of the figures of *com-media* both to play upon the most immediate and direct emotional situations and relationships and to celebrate the theatrical artifice of those very actions. This ability is the source of the power of the Harle-quins of Blok and Meyerhold and of Evreinov. Less directly but no less knowingly, it is the source of the theatre-within-theatre power of the strange pageant of Pirandello's Enrico, whose madness becomes con-scious artifice—but still, in the end, traps him murderously in his mask of madness. It is there in the carefully framed, self-consciously theatrical master-slave insanity of Beckett's Pozzo and Lucky. Indeed, Lucky's great monologue, full of the fractured rhetoric of deep sentiment and dan-gerous thought—and the desperate avoidance thereof—is arguably a descendant of a *commedia tirate,* its ninety-odd lines a bravura expatia-tion upon and simultaneous demonstration of our existential disposses-sion.

The agendas of the modernists, in all their revolutionary variety, were in some ways not that different from those of Fo and Schumann—at least they also sought a theatre that was more than theatre, that actually made a difference in the world's consciousness of itself. It is not surpris-ing, then, that they all turned to a form of theatre that gave them models for both direct dramatic communication and layered artifice. It is not necessary—in fact it is not even possible—to make the argument that there are definitive connections between the *lazzi* and the scenarios and even the characters of the original *commedia dell'arte* and their twentieth-century descendants. The Russian critic Boris Asaf'yev once described the legacy of Italian melody as "a kind of universal reserve—a musical 'central heating system'" for European music (1982, 188). I would argue that this description is as true for Italian popular theatre as for Italian popular melody, but it would be nothing but a sweeping banality if it carried no specific weight. Asaf'yev applied his metaphor to the music of Stravinski, illuminating thereby the particular tenderness and warm plasticity of his treatment of Pergolesi and other Baroque Italians in the still distinctly modern *commedia*, *Pulcinella*. Similarly, it is possible to see the panoply of *commedia* figures and techniques as a source of energy and liberation to those who rediscovered them in the theatre.

One of the common but nonetheless striking features of the sequences of *commedia* plot is their marvelous outlandishness, their sovereign disregard of limitations. There is no dead end that cannot be solved with a timely coincidence or sleight of hand or handy disguise. There is no limit to the level of complication caused, and resolved, by creative misunderstanding and indirection. Doralice of *Innocence Restored* experiences the full spectrum of trickery, false accusation, near murder, rise to power, and redemption, all at a dizzying pace made dizzier by the *lazzi* and improvisations that glue it all together. To return to the theme of the "central heating system," it is not necessary to make specific claims of influence to detect the flow of warmth into a number of different heated imaginations—granting that the *scenari* were themselves often adapted from other sources, including the learned comedies and *their* sources, but also insisting that this adaptation makes no difference, since it is by way of the *commedia dell'arte* that these plots moved through history. For instance, and to make one relatively specific claim, is it not possible that *Innocence Restored* is a distant model of the internalized and domesticated, mental extravagance of suspicion, disbelief, and ironic exposure in Pirandello's *It Is So (If You Think So)*, another tale of a wronged woman, after all?

A more extroverted version of this heated extravagance is present in Jarry, and in Genet's *clownerie*, *The Blacks*, to very different effect. Changing gears, it is there in any number of epic plots in slapstick comedy, and in such Marx brothers' masterpieces of controlled anarchy as *A Night at the Opera*—and in the works of movie comedy, and even the cumulative absurdity of Ionesco, who with a bow to the Surrealists, still claimed that the greatest influences upon him were Groucho, Chico, and Harpo Marx (Esslin 1961, 237).

But these examples are just more of the endless chatter about influence to which *commedia* devotees are addicted. The point is that the *commedia dell'arte* gave its successors a gift of freedom to be grotesque, to be errant, to burst boundaries of character and situation—all, returning to the rule of paradox, within a pattern that restores order and returns to the always visible frame of the theatre. To the modernists and to our contemporary masters of social and dramatic revolution, any claims of personal freedom in a world ruled by big corporations, big government, and big media are either suspect or laden with a necessary call to subversion. As Fo and Schumann have expressed in their different ways, the artist who would serve the cause of freedom has the double problem of avoiding castration and finding a truly potent language of subversion. They and their predecessors have found at least a portion of the tools they need in the tricks of the *commedia* trade. Isabella's madness flaring through the convolutions of a labyrinthine plot gives license—a legacy of legitimacy from the triumphantly illegitimate—to all those who would make a new drama to cure a mad world.

Works Cited

Asaf'yev, Boris. *A Book about Stravinsky.* Translated by Richard French. Ann Arbor: UMI Research Press, 1982.

Esslin, Martin. *The Theatre of the Absurd.* New York: Doubleday, 1961.

Farrell, Joseph. "Dario Fo—Zanni and Giullare." In *The* Commedia dell'Arte *from the Renaissance to Dario Fo,* edited by Christopher Cairns, 315–28. Lewiston: Edwin Mellen Press, 1989.

Jenkins, Ron. "Clowns, Politics and Miracles: The Epic Satire of Dario Fo." *American Theatre* 3:3 (June 1986): 10–16.

———. "Reagan's Last Laugh: Supply-Side Comedy and the Americanization of Arlecchino." In Commedia dell'Arte *and the Comic Spirit,* edited by Michael Bigelow Dixon and Michelle Y. Togami, 47–52. Louisville, KY: Actors Theatre of Louisville, 1990.

Rame, Franca. "Introduction." In *We Can't Pay? We Won't Pay!,* by Dario Fo, translated by Lino Pertile. London: Pluto Press, 1978.

Rudnitsky, Konstantin. *Meyerhold the Director.* Translated by George Petrov. Edited by Sydney Schultze. Ann Arbor, MI: Ardis, 1981.

Schumann, Peter. *The Radicality of the Puppet Theatre.* Glover, VT: Bread and Puppet Theatre, 1991.

A Semiotic Perspective on

the *Commedia dell'Arte*

Michael L. Quinn

*M*Y CONTRIBUTION will not offer any new information about the *commedia dell'arte* as such, but will propose a sensible approach to its explanation. Scholars have always supposed that the acting companies that produced the *commedia* performances had to carry out their business with a clear mutual understanding of the narrative materials and procedural techniques of their performances. The "textuality" of these performances treads a narrow path between plan and improvisation, which is one of the most fascinating aspects of the *commedia* form, at least from the perspective of a contemporary theatre that is still, despite an intense period of modernist experiment, largely dominated by a text-based model of theatre production. I think this habitual concern with the text has tended to distract modern scholars and directors from the other techniques through which performances were planned, and it seems to me that the easiest way to establish the communication systems through which the performances were controlled is through the use of a semiotic perspective.

The Prospects for Semiotic Explanation

Semiotics draws its approach from language, since it tends to conceive of all communication through principles of similarity and difference that were first developed in linguistic fields like phonology. The strength of semiotics in relation to the *commedia* is the way it can describe how non-linguistic aspects of the performances participate as signs in systems of communication that operate "like language," creating meanings that are every bit as specific and clear as those communicated by a text of written dialogues. Since semiotics has no value in and of itself, but must be judged by its ability to generate explanations of an acceptable scope and precision, I'd like to approach the semiotics of the *commedia* from a couple of different directions, and see what we can find in the symposium readings that bears out the value of a systematic look at signs in the theatre.

Scenarios and the Perspective of Culture

Broadly conceived, semiotics proposes to explain the entire cultural system of communication, including the terms of sign exchange within a cultural context, the ways those exchanges can be disrupted to confound communication, and the terms through which the cultural system attempts to account for things and events that fall largely outside its cultural framework. This cultural perspective, then, does not suggest that it is impossible to understand another culture, but that it may be difficult to do so; the culture of *commedia*, so far removed from contemporary life, presents a considerable challenge to the interpretive imagination.

Perhaps the easiest way to see how signs function in the general culture is to notice the way they are exchanged in the performances, as these moments are documented in the scenarios and reports. A clear example is in the report of Pavoni's diary on a *Madness of Isabella* performance, in which the spectator writes of Fileno and Isabella's elopement that "they planned the flight for the evening, agreeing between them signs which would make each known to the other" (Richards and Richards 1990, 75). Of course these signs were a matter of private agreement, not part of the cultural system as such, except that they are instantly projected into a cultural situation when they are overheard by Fileno's rival, Flavio. We are then told that "at the agreed time, or rather shortly before it, Flavio appeared and made his presence known by way of the signs Fileno was due to give to Isabella. Isabella immediately came out of the house and was met by Flavio with a delight beyond imagining" (Richards and Richards 1990, 75). The private signs were meant to establish terms for a private relation between two lovers, but they were immediately penetrated and appropriated by someone who knew that they had been developed as a substitute for ordinary, socially legitimate matrimonial vows. Here signs serve as a theme in the play scenarios, much in the way they did in one of the first books to use semiotics to interpret dramatic literature, Suzanne Relyea's 1976 study of Molière's comedies, *Signs, Systems and Meanings*, which proposed that semiotics is precisely that in which Molière's husbands, wives, and bourgeois gentlemen are schooled.

Of course signs are not only matters of private agreement, but of agreement generally, thereby providing the vehicles of social institutions like marriage, business partnerships, vows of friendship, or bonds of servitude. Often in the *commedia dell'arte* scenarios, for example, people give their words as their bonds, or give some symbolic token of a promise. Conventional sign exchange is so extensive, so heavily relied upon by the people in the performed stories, that signs often constitute a kind of material proof, though of course oaths and objects are still signs that can sometimes be manipulated. Rings serve as signs, for example, in *Innocence Restored,* where they signify the faithfulness of Doralice and Horatio to their betrothal. When Fabritio is able to steal her ring, it serves as a false proof of Doralice's unfaithfulness, for he is able to corroborate this evidence of betrayal with an even more personal sign of his intimacy, his report of the sight of a mole under her breast. In the same play, Zanni is inspired by the gift of Fabritio's chain to imitate the manners of a gentleman; here the golden chain implies false signs of social class that he sends out while rehearsing his rise in society; finally these false signs of status only serve to communicate to a thief that Zanni has joined the class of appropriate crime victims. The ideas of mistaken identity and disguise, so basic to the action of almost every *commedia* performance, are regular aspects of the *commedia*'s form, in which signs of even the most basic social agreements (like identity, sex, and class) are consciously "at risk" in the story, though usually so only to be confirmed by the final resolution of the plot into a series of marriages. At the conclusion of *Innocence Restored,* when the complicated knot of family relations and romantic obligations is finally untangled, the summary lesson of the performance might well be that, contrary to our general assumption that ordinary, often arbitrarily conceived signs of social standing and proof are true, appearances are not always what they seem to be; conventional social signs like names can sometimes obscure such physical signs as family resemblance, and supposed proofs of intimacy may not always imply a romantic episode that both parties shared.

Consequently the scenarios, from a cultural perspective, are not only broadly semiotic, but also sometimes even consciously "anti-semiotic." In this larger view, signs are more than mere media of social interaction; they often actually constitute the cultural situations within which they work. Consider, for example, the situation of the Turk in *Innocence Restored.* Foreign characters usually exist at the edge of a cultural system, and this Turk is no exception; he comes ashore during an act of war and hopes to find refuge in a country that has been established as hostile ground. His "otherness" in the system grants him special knowledge—

he knows how to cure the royal gout—and a dangerous strangeness. The Turk wears women's clothes; we suppose that he is murdered by chance, but Horatio is strangely immune from prosecution from his supposed murder of Doralice because his victim was only a fugitive foreigner. Isabella's situation in the scenario named for her madness similarly dramatizes the strange boundaries of the cultural system; imagine, for example, that the situation were reversed—that Isabella was an Italian wife who ran away with a Muslim, later killed her Italian child and husband, and then coverted to Islam, tried to kill another man, and went crazy when a Muslim wedding was denied to her. Could such a person survive as a heroine in an Italian *commedia* scenario? Probably not. The foreigner's liminality helps in these cases to constitute a cultural "inside."

Another perspective on the coherence of a cultural system of signs comes in the scenarios' many scenes of madness or delirium. The use of nonsense in the plays only makes us more aware that the ordinary ways of making sense in a culture depend upon memory, upon a mastery of communicative codes, and upon sincere expression. Isabella's madness in the Scala scenario is part of her "otherness"; she does not fit in, does not understand her husband's behavior, and in a crucial moment the whole system of signs breaks down in her mind—she is awake, but has lost "semiotic consciousness." The audience knows she is mad because they know how sense gets made in their culture, and they can tell she is not making any.

Madness is not purely practical, however; in *The Enchanted Wood*, madness is an aesthetic effect of magic. Fillide and Sireno, when they eat the apples, are strangely abstracted from the coherence of the world of signs; they know some words, and say some really fascinating things, but their madess is a virtuosic failure of memory and communicative competence, which we read by their signs. Magical transport, like cultural otherness, puts the semiotic system under some strain, but in the process it reveals the fascinating workings of the mind and the fragility of society. Whether placed as characters outside a society, like the Savage, or above it, like Sabino the magician, both kinds of strangers establish the semiotic boundaries of the world of the *commedia dell'arte* and allow us to marvel at its workings. Spectators are not trapped within these dramatic boundaries, for the performances help them to perceive social limits as such, testing a potential for broader understanding. And from the perspective of a semiotic aesthetics, effects of magic and delirium are especially interesting because the easy, everyday senses of signs are made strange, and they begin to be perceived imaginatively, as occasions for the experience of beauty.

Commedia Performance as an Artistic System

Another way to look at the *commedia*'s signs is to suspend consideration of the world *commedia* tries to show and to consider instead the way
that it shows the world, to view the images, ideas, and techniques of the
commedia as a kind of systematic artistic language. From this perspective
it is crucial to keep in mind that semiotic systems are not just dead, fixed
codes, but dynamic, changeable processes for the creative generation of
an infinite number of expressive combinations of signs.

What are these signs? The *commedia dell'arte* is an especially challeng-
ing semiotic system because its textuality is suppressed; it is harder to
reduce its meanings to a set of literary themes in the way that Northrup
Frye, for example, codified literature through the organization of its
principal narratives and images. Yet the *commedia dell'arte* clearly exists
within an "inter-textual" network of resemblances and associations with
other texts that influence its meanings; we would not be comparing *The
Enchanted Wood* to *The Tempest* if this sort of semiotic association of
coded elements were not part of the way the *commedia* generates its
meanings. Rather than viewing this inter-text as some supposed lack of
originality, we might consider that the network of associations provides a
background of shared understanding, against which extremely complex
dramatic actions and amazingly novel expressions can emerge in performance. Shakespeare's involvement with ten volumes of narrative and
dramatic sources does not seem to dampen our impression of his originality, and in the *commedia dell'arte* this sort of background system could
be adapted by a skilled improvisational company for every single performance. The transformations of *The Enchanted Wood* are clearly indebted
to Ovid, yet their place within the scenario itself is also unique. Stage
images and actions, then, like their literary analogues, have a systematic
character in the *commedia dell'arte*.

The most obvious system of signs is the set of acting figures in the
company, the system of masks and stock character images. Not only is
this system dynamic, as anyone can see from the marvelous variety of
situations that these characters can produce, but also it provides a won-
derful security for the whole structure of the drama. One of the basic
assumptions of semiotic aesthetics is the idea that novelty is only percep-
tible for an audience against a background of orienting norms, a set of
ordinary expectations that provides the context for invention. The stage
figures of the *commedia* characters, combined with a variety of antecedent
narratives, scenic possibilites, and standard patterns of desire, are much
more constant and reliable than the action itself, much more predictable

than the twists and turns of the plot, which is in most cases designed to produce contradiction and surprise. The repeating characters provide the primary context for spectator recognition, radically different from the artistic situation of the scripted drama of the English and Spanish Renaissance theatre, which would invent new characters for every text. This dependability of the characters increases the confidence of audience identifications; consequently, the actors could depend upon a strong empathy from the audience that allowed them—perhaps even encouraged them—to take creative risks. The images were so stable that they provided the structural basis for the scenarios, and even inspired systems of character in other artistic forms, such as genre painting or pantomime. The characters' stage figures, then, are basic signs, the building blocks of *commedia* semiotics; they differed from company to company, so that in some troupes a woman like Argentina or Isabella might dominate the repertory, while in others the leader would be a *zanni* like Fiorello's Scaramouche, but in each case they provide a strong theatrical link that could hold a divergent repertory of performances together.

There is a tendency, however, to suppose that the visual images alone were the constitutive aspects of the *commedia* characters—perhaps an unavoidable result of the lack of vivid performance records as opposed to the wealth of visual evidence on the *commedia*. Yet the vitality of the form was surely in the principles of action, the combinations of set speeches and patterns of improvisation that expressed the characteristic motivations of the masks in specific situations. The *zibaldone* record what we know of this lively art, the sorts of set speeches like tirades or rodomontades that were learned as interchangeable parts of the dramas, the *lazzi* that could be introduced to animate any number of scenes, the supplements of music or scenic effect, and the patterns of improvised comment on a metaphor or a conventional sign—love's fire, a white handkerchief, etc.—that emerge in amorous dialogues like those excerpted from Perrucci. This principle of action suggests a semiotics that is not made of stable subjects, but of lively predicates, a system that never rests because it is designed for the constant advancement of a transformational artistic style, a pragmatics of theatrical performance.

The Historical Situation

These transformations assure us that the *commedia* was more than a passive reflection of social states of affairs and was in fact an active agent of their exploration and transformation. From this standpoint the agents of repression who denounced the *commedia* were quite right to be anxious about what it taught; despite its historicity, the lively adaptability of the *commedia* actors to sharp swings in situation was a training ground for skilled social beings, not a vapid entertainment designed to reinforce the status quo. Of the scenarios the symposium has considered, most are driven by female desire, or by a love that seems to challenge the status quo of profitable marriages arranged within the appropriate class. Conservatives and reactionaries had little use for *commedia* precisely because the semiotic principles of its organization ensured that the form would have little for them. So long as comedy is based in contradictory perceptions and surprise, proponents of uniformity will find occasions to object; this generic predilection of the *commedia* system is consequently the one that Barbieri is at the most pains to defend, and which he tries hard to describe as a minor effect of the art, merely one among many (Richards and Richards, 1990, 253–54).

Perhaps the most interesting section in the readings is the part on the English attitudes toward *commedia* (Richards and Richards 1990, 274–78), because it brings the two aspects of semiotics that I have described—cultural and artistic—together into a clear case of intercultural theatre contact. The early English, like Kemp, sought to characterize the Italian system as depraved; the women must be whores, and the actors of Harlequin equal to the stupidity of their character. Yet Fiorello established such a reputation that the Restoration monarch brought him from Paris for special performances; the clown, like the Turk, is both a monstrous other and a holder of special knowledge. In this case the monstrosity and the knowledge are both matters of sheer artistic skill; moreover, Fiorello was a master of intercultural performance. Having managed to entertain French crowds in Italian for many years, he was more than equal to the task of adapting his style to the tastes of yet another foreign-language audience. Indeed, the constructive effect of stable character images and traits renders the role of language considerably less crucial to communication than other dramatic forms (as music cancels text in opera), while the context of a foreign language invites delicious uses for the many scenes of linguistic delirium, when unexpected resemblances between the languages could be discovered to delightful effect.

Conclusion

I have suggested the outlines of a semiotic perspective on the *commedia*. Certainly the idea of several different sign systems, all relatively equal, relieves the *commedia* form of much of its anxiety about literature, but I think semiotics is also a useful tool for the historical interpretation of *commedia* performance problems, and especially for the study of the problems of intercultural translation that make *commedia* difficult to imagine in relation to the contemporary moment, and harder still to revive.

Works Cited

Frye, Northrop. *Anatomy of Criticism: Four Essays*. Princeton, NJ: Princeton University Press, 1957.

Relyea, Suzanne. *Signs, Systems, and Meanings: A Contemporary Semiotic Reading of Four Molière Plays*. Middletown, CT: Wesleyan University Press, 1976.

Richards, Kenneth, and Laura Richards. *The* Commedia dell'Arte: *A Documentary History*. Oxford: Shakespeare Head Press, 1990.

Commedia dell'Arte and the

Spanish Golden Age Theatre

Nancy L. D'Antuono

*M*Y AREA OF EXPERTISE is the relationship between the *commedia dell'arte* and the theatre of Spain's Golden Age. Early in my academic career I began working with the Italian *novella* and its presence in the theatre of Lope de Vega. As I examined the thirty-two Lope plays derived from Italian short stories, I became reacquainted with the *commedia dell'arte* and its role in shaping Lope's dramaturgy in general, and in particular the eight plays examined in detail. About twelve years ago, at a conference in Rome, a fellow *comedia* specialist suggested that I look into the presence of the Spanish *comedia* in Italy during the seventeenth century and its impact on Italian dramaturgy, both as concerns the *commedia erudita* or *sostenuta* and the *commedia dell'arte*. As I proceeded with my research I ran into a critical stance on the part of Italian scholars which paralleled that of scholars treating Spanish Golden Age plays. Only a few plays met the high standards of these critics as concerned content. Most of the *rifacimenti* of Spanish plays were written off as neither fish nor fowl and barely worthy of discussion. As for the Spanish repertory of the *commedia dell'arte*—nary a word. The rigidity of posture reminded me of my undergraduate and graduate courses in Spanish drama in which the same "sacred" plays were discussed over and over again as the masterpieces of Spain's seventeenth-century theatre. Among these were *El médico de su honra (The Surgeon of His Honor)*, in which a husband has his wife bled to death to prevent his "honor" from being tarnished by the prince's unwelcome attentions; *Fuenteovejuna (The Sheepwell)*, which treats the themes of the responsibility of rulers and the respect for human dignity no matter what the social class; and *La* *vida es sueño (Life Is a Dream),* which deals with the question of man's comportment in this world if, indeed, it is but a dream. Rarely did we read a comic play. I can recall only one, *Don Gil de las calzas verdes (Don Gil of the Green Stockings).* Yet when one considers the immense popularity of the Spanish *comedia* at home and in Italy (under Spanish domination from 1504 until 1700) and the vast quantity of plays that reached the boards of both nations, how can it be that so few plays emerge as representative masterpieces? If all of the others are, by implication, so imperfect, how do we account for their unqualified success as Spanish stage pieces and their subsequent triumph as Italian *rifacimenti* and *commedia dell'arte scenari?* I mention both genres together since I believe them to be one and the same, theatrically speaking, with common roots and much interdependence in the evolution of their form, if not their content.

Performing in Spain between 1574 and 1597, the *comici dell'arte* contributed directly to the evolution of the Spanish *comedia* and to the development of the *gracioso,* perfected by Lope de Vega from *zanni.* Lope's fascination with the *commedia dell'arte* and its masks and its *lazzi* has been well documented. His plays contain numerous references to the masks and antics of Ganassa, Arlecchino, Stefanello Bottarga, Trastullo, and Franceschina. Lope attended the *commedia dell'arte* performances with such regularity that he was once arrested for libel while sitting at a performance of *los italianos.* In 1599 we find him in Valencia, leading a Carnival parade dressed in the red and black garb of Pantalone. Having come to Spain when its national theatre was just taking shape, the *comici* offered Lope de Vega, and through him all subsequent Golden Age dramatists, those elements that would characterize Spanish stage offerings of the next hundred years: a three-act dramatic structure, balance and duplication in plot and characterization, and a rapid-moving story line centering on the tribulations of young lovers who, with the help of crafty servants, outwit rivals and elders in order to bring their love to fruition. The Spaniards would repay this debt some fifty years later by providing the *comici dell'arte* with new plots with which to shore up their waning repertory.

Before I discuss the *commedia dell'arte*'s approach to the Spanish comedies, some comment is necessary as to the content of the Spanish sources. The dramatic energy of these pieces stems from the playwright's ability to fuse the theatrical novelties of the Italian players to the social, ideological, and religious mandates of his age. The emerging comedies are cohesive units that, while thoroughly entertaining, reaffirm, or at least appear to affirm, three givens: Church, Monarchy, and Honor. I would mention, parenthetically, that the last two elements—the monarchical ideal and the Spanish code of honor—were the components with which Italian *rifacitori* and *capocomici* had the greatest difficulty. In fact, the subtle logic of the Spanish honor code was to a large degree incomprehensible to the Italians.

The *commedia dell'arte*'s unrivaled capacity for revitalization and accommodation brought the actors, out of necessity, to the Spanish *comedia*. By the end of the first quarter of the seventeenth century the Italian repertory had worn thin from repetition (they had, after all, been kings of the boards for over sixty years). Their audience was now being seduced by a competing force: the *comedia* of Lope and his followers as performed by Spanish acting troupes pouring into viceregal Naples and from there to ambassadorial courts in Rome, Florence, Mantua, Milano, and Venice. By 1630 Naples' *Via del Teatro dei Fiorentini* had already been renamed (at least by reputation) *Via della commedia spagnola*. The *comici* had no choice but to take to themselves what they recognized as the latest craving of their public. The spectators' demands and the *comici*'s obeisance kept the Spanish *comedia* on the Italian stage until the end of the eighteenth century. Who better to ensure the longevity of the *commedia dell'arte* than the very art form it had helped shape half a century earlier? They had before them a wealth of plays whose success was undeniable. Lope and his followers offered works that incorporated the best of the *commedia dell'arte* while eliminating the gross language and obscene gestures that antagonized church authorities. How could the *comici* resist?

The Italian players' interest in the Spanish *comedia* went beyond the sudden quest for new material and financial gain. The relationship between the actors of the two nations had been nurtured by mutual esteem for each others' talents. Italian actors felt much could be learned from the Spaniards' execution of serious roles; Spaniards admired the *comici*'s ability to create while performing. Spanish and Italian actors had worked side by side since the arrival of the first Spanish performers in 1620. The company of Antonio de Melo, a Portuguese Neapolitan who made his career on the stage as Captain Flegetonte, included two Spanish actors. The positive reaction of the Italian audience to the *entr'acte* dancing of Beatriz de Guzmán prompted de Melo to offer next Spanish cape-and-sword plays. Both Spaniards and Italians reacted so well that de Melo encouraged Sancho de Paz to form a regular company for the following season. Thus began a symbiotic relationship that was to last at least one hundred years. A contract of 1620 lists two Italian actors with Sancho de Paz. They were Ambrosio Buonhomo (Coviello) and Andrea Calcese (Pulcinella), who played out their well-known *contrasti* during the *intermezzi*. In 1621 a third Italian joined them: Bartolomeo Ziti, who played a Neapolitan Dottor Gratiano. In 1628 he was still part of the company and traveled to Rome with them. Artistic commonality transcended national and linguistic barriers. The rich professional cross-fertilization and the longstanding respect for one another's art coupled with unequivocal acclaim led naturally to the assimilation of Spanish plots into the Italian repertory. Spanish play texts circulated freely among them, often long before the works were published in Spain. A case in point is the scenario *Sette infanti dell'Ara* (Codex XI AA.40, Biblioteca Nazionale, Naples). A letter by the actress Leonora Castiglione mentions its being performed during the 1634 season, yet the source play, Lope de Vega's *El Bastardo Mudarra,* was not published until 1641.

The absorption of Spanish plays into the Italian repertory brought with it another phenomenon: the translation for publication of Spanish plays by Italian actors and actresses. The earliest on record are those of Marco Napolione, an actor who flourished around the middle of the seventeenth century and was famous for the role of Flaminio. Unfortunately, Napolione's twenty-two translations, the titles of which are recorded in Allacci's *Dramaturgia* (1655), are no longer extant. By 1676 Angela D'Orso, in the service of the Duke of Modena, had translated twelve Spanish plays, four of which are extant. Domenico Antonio Parrino, the actor-turned-publisher (known for the role of Flaminio in late seventeenth-century Naples), printed works translated by fellow actors. There are extant translations by Orsola Biancolelli (wife of the famous seventeenth-century Arlecchino, Domenico Biancolelli), Francesco Manzani, Nicolo Biancolelli, and Francesco Calderoni. The tradition continues in the eighteenth century with the translations of Francesco Bartoli, Luigi Riccoboni, and D. Placido Adriani. As for the reason for these translations, I can only surmise that the actors had probably played the leading roles on stage or translated the work at the request of a noble patron and subsequently decided to publish the translation, thereby legitimizing their function as quasi-*literati* rather than simply as actors and actresses.

The plays most commonly adapted or translated by the *comici* were the lighthearted comedies of intrigue, those which most resembled the typical *commedia dell'arte* offerings. The tripartite structure common to both art forms facilitated the transposition of content *grosso modo,* but did not preclude adjustments stemming from a particular *capocomico's* dramatic vision. Here, too, the rearrangement was easily accomplished. The *galán* and *dama* of the Spanish original became the *primo innamorato and prima donna* of the Italian company. Similarly, the second pair of lovers (if the subplot so demanded) could be passed on to the second lover and second lady. The blocking figure, if a parent, might now be Pantalone or Dottor Gratiano. If the Spanish plot contained an unsuccessful second suitor, the role most often went to the Capitano. The *dama*'s female servant found her counterpart in the *servetta;* the *gracioso* easily reverted back to his progenitor, Zanni and variants thereof. As for the scenario's title, the *comici* simply translated the Spanish into parallel Italian phrases. There was no effort to hide the source. In fact, they banked on the audience's recognition of the piece in order to draw a large crowd. They also knew that plays by Lope de Vega drew the largest audiences and did not hesitate to place his name on their publicity posters even when the work was not his.

The preference for comedies of intrigue did not exclude the occasional adaptation of tragic or serious pieces. The *comici* recognized the dramatic power of these works and of their audience appeal. The adaptations, however, while adhering to the Spanish plot lines, often scene by scene, are testaments to the divergent social values of both nations. For example, in the case of *Il medico di suo honore* (Ms. 4186, Biblioteca Casanatense, Rome, from Calderón's *Médico de su honra,* mentioned above), the ending of the play was recast twice, pointing to the discomfort of the Italians with the murder (by bleeding) of an innocent wife for the sake of one's "honor." The notion of a husband standing around congratulating himself over the clever manner in which he had avoided defamation was simply more than an Italian audience could tolerate. It could accept the death of an adulterous spouse, but not the premeditated elimination of a guiltless woman. Whereas the king in Calderón's play is reluctant to punish the offending husband, in the first of the Italian revisions the king condemns the man to death. The king subsequently spares him owing to the supplications of many members of the court as well as those of a lady who loves the protagonist. Marked for insertion at the point where the lady and the members of the court plead for the husband's life is a second revised ending. The king now asks for time to reconsider the death penalty. Witnesses, including the man who had attempted to seduce her, come forth to attest to the wife's innocence. Accepting their testimony as fact, the king decides that the husband must die and invites all to attend the execution. Thus the protagonist's execution is an unavoidable act of justice stemming from the rational examination of facts.

By and large, however, the comedies of intrigue that ended with one or more couples happily married were the favorites of the *comici*. To date 104 *scenari* have been traced to Spanish sources. Of these, seven are my own discoveries in the course of my research on the theatres of Calderón and Lope de Vega in Italy. As I worked with the three new pieces deriving from Lope's theatre, an interesting phenomenon emerged. Each of the Spanish plays was derived from an Italian *novella*. Thus we find the Italians recapturing their own literary heritage through a Spanish literary filter. My study confirms that each of the three *scenari* is clearly derived from the Spanish and not from the original *novella*. This finding, in turn, raises another issue. We know that the *novella* by its very structure lent itself to dramatization and that it is likely that many *novelle* found their way into the *commedia dell'arte* repertory. This fact brings me to a question Tom Heck raised: How can we be sure that Lope was not inspired in each instance, at least partially, by an earlier Italian scenario? The possibility cannot be discounted. Unfortunately, none of the sixteenth-century pieces have survived. To date I have come across only one play that strongly suggests such a possibility. I refer to Calderón's *El alcaide de si mismo (The Jailer of Himself)*, which subsequently appears as a scenario, *Guardia de se stesso* (Codex XI AA.40, dated 1700, Biblioteca Nazionale, Naples). Although there are Italian nobles in the Spanish play, the most important character seems to be Benito, a country bumpkin who finds a suit of armor (discarded by a fleeing nobleman), puts it on, and is then arrested. His captors believe him to be the Prince of Sicily who has recently killed another Italian nobleman in a tournament. Benito, as "Prince," is detained, and a substantial portion of the remainder of the play centers on the humorous episodes arising from the differing perceptions by the other characters of the uncouth "Prince." In the Naples scenario, Benito is Pulcinella, who differs little from his Spanish predecessor except in his preference for *maccheroni* when offered food. If anything, Calderón's Benito appears to be more of a glutton than Pulcinella himself. In relation to the other characters, Benito's role assumes a great deal more importance than is common in these plays. Although I have not yet been able to pinpoint an Italian source, I remain convinced, since the setting is Naples and the characters are mostly Italian nobles, and in view of the Benito/Pulcinella parallel, that an earlier scenario may indeed have inspired Calderón's play.

The same may be true, though to a much lesser extent, in the case of two Lope plays related to two of the *scenari* under consideration here. Before approaching these, I would like to call attention to Lope de Vega's high regard for Isabella Andreini, *prima donna* of *The Madness of Isabella*. She is mentioned in two of his last plays, *El castigo sin venganza* (1632) and *Las bizarrias de Belisa* (1634). In the first play the Duke of Ferrara, eager for a night of merrymaking, sets out with his servants to find an appropriate place. They come to a door and hear some actors rehearsing. The Duke comments that if it is Andrelina (a misspelling of "la Andreini") she is an actress of great fame, capable of displaying many extremes of emotion. In the second comedy, the heroine Belisa recites a sonnet. The gentleman with her remarks that it is worthy of "Isabella Andreina," such is its beauty. I have not yet been able to confirm whether Lope actually saw Isabella Andreini perform or whether he knew her only by reputation, possibly through his contact with Italians in Madrid, Seville, or Valencia. There is no record of the Andreinis having performed in Spain, although there is a document in the Archives of Seville that refers to a Spanish company of actors known as *Los celosos*. Is this name a deliberate attempt to recall *I Gelosi*? Had the Spaniards seen them perform and modeled their company after theirs? Until more documents surface, the question must remain unanswered.

Lope may have intended to honor Isabella Andreini and also Francesco in an early comedy, *La discreta enamorada* (1606–1608). It is a play in which the presence of the *commedia dell'arte* is almost palpable, in my opinion. In its comic vitality, its sparkling dialogue, and its swift forward thrust of the action, the work corresponds closely to the kind of intrigues for which the Italian players were famous. The plot advances almost entirely on the basis of deceptions, tricks, and jokes perpetrated by the principal characters on one another. Although the setting is Spanish, there appears to be little concern for the question of honor. The question of the protagonist's nobility, usually inseparable from matters of honor, is conspicuously absent. The characters—the lovers aside—all seem more concerned with the accumulation of wealth than with values of any transcendence. Though Spanish in name, the characters appear to be adaptations of Italian prototypes. Beyond the *zanni/gracioso, innamorati/ enamorados* parallels, Lope's Captain Bernardo is a brilliant fusion of the braggart Captain and Pantalone. He is the robust, middle-aged father and retired soldier eager to marry a spirited young girl, Fenisa—young enough to marry his son, whom the girl really loves. The close ties between the role of the Captain and that of Fenisa, who once having accepted his proposal of marriage orchestrates the foolish Captain's every move until she emerges married to the man of her choice, prompts me to think of Francesco Andreini (Capitano Spavento) and of his wife, Isabella, *prima donna* of the troupe. Could not the Italian acting couple and the roles they immortalized have suggested the characterization of the corresponding roles in *La discreta enamorada*? Isabella died in France on June 11, 1605, and shortly thereafter Francesco retired from the stage. Lope's play was written between 1606 and 1608. Had Lope intended to honor their memory in *La discreta enamorada*? I believe so. The fact that Lope pays unmistakable tribute to the famous acting talents of Isabella three decades later in two of his last plays would seem to support the hypothesis.

As for the scenari, *The Madness of Isabella* and *Innocence Restored*, these may be connected to two plays by Lope de Vega—*Los locos de Valencia* (*The Mad Ones of Valencia*, written between 1590 and 1595) and *Viuda, casada y doncella* (*Married, Widowed and Chaste*, 1595–1603)—though not in the usual linear fashion. Lope seems to have taken the notion of a lady going mad upon finding herself rejected and expanded upon it to include three characters who feign madness to be near the one they love whom they believe to be mad. Beyond the notion of madness caused by abandonment by one's beloved, the plots move in different directions. Interestingly enough, the plot of *Viuda, casada y doncella* has several points in common with *The Madness of Isabella*, yet its title is thematically tied to *Innocence Restored* (1622) and the matter of the lady's gout being cured by one who is "married, widowed, yet a virgin." In both *Madness* and *Viuda* we have a lover who is shipwrecked in Moorish waters. In both, the man becomes attached to a Moorish girl who is willing to betray her master to run off with her new love. In *Madness*, Oratio eventually marries Isabella; in *Viuda*, once the escape has been effected, Floriano tells Fátima that he is married to Clavela and that he cannot marry her. Fátima settles for marrying Celio, Floriano's manservant, when the latter asks for her hand. Oratio's and Floriano's absence encourages the pursuit of their ladies by rivals. The endings, however, veer in different directions. Horatio recognizes his obligation to Isabella and marries her; Floriano arrives just in time to stop the union of Liberio and Clavela and claims Clavela as his wife.

As for the ties between *Viuda, casada y doncella* and *Innocence Restored*, they do not go much beyond the title. Lope's chaste widow has no magic power to cure maladies. Since Lope's play predates the Locatelli scenario (1622)—it also predates Verucci's *Il Dispettoso Marito* (1612)— might Lope's play have inspired Verucci's play or the Locatelli scenario? It would not seem so. Perhaps it would be more appropriate to say, in this instance, that they both deal with a theme common to both the folklore and the *novella* tradition.

The Influence of

Commedia dell'Arte Scenari

on the Modern Stage

James Fisher

DWARD GORDON CRAIG wrote in 1912 that "in the *commedia dell'arte* the Italians of the late sixteenth century gave to future generations a hint as to the possibilities of the Art of the Theatre" (104). Surveying the proliferation of *commedia*-inspired works produced in the twentieth century, one can only suspect that Craig himself might well be astonished at how broadly this "hint" has been taken.

Two scenarios made available for this symposium, *Innocence Restored* and *The Madness of Isabella*, offer, as most surviving scenarios do, a vivid sense of the style of *commedia*. Beyond that, *Innocence Restored* gives us a scenario with significant literary descendants, while *The Madness of Isabella* offers a highly representative plot and characters. These aspects of *commedia* scenarios and traditions had significant influence on Craig and a staggeringly diverse group of his contemporaries, as well as on subsequent generations of theatrical artists. It seems important to note here that *commedia* is a performance tradition; to study the scenarios as literature is certainly an illuminating exercise, but only recovers one aspect of *commedia*. The scenarios must be regarded as tools for performance, and only one kind of tool.

What seems to be critical in understanding the ways in which these scenarios and *commedia* in general have influenced twentieth-century theatre is the realization that each individual modern artist has viewed *commedia* traditions and techniques in unique, highly selective, and often quite inaccurate ways. However, some general notions of *commedia* seem to be present in most twentieth-century artists.

First, these artists noted that *commedia dell'arte* was the rarest of theatrical forms—a nonliterary theatre that emphasized the skill of the improvising actor. They observed that *commedia* actors, in their stock roles and through the vehicle supplied by the scenarios, transformed human folly and vice into incisive satire. Modern *commedia*-inspired artists could look at surviving scenarios and see their value as inspiration. Craig, for one, studied *commedia* scenarios and found them illuminating. He wrote in his journal, *The Mask,* that *commedia* scenarios made the plays of literary dramatists such as Shakespeare and George Bernard Shaw seem unnecessarily restrictive because they required little from the actor or director, and "did not inspire me to create. But the bare framework of 'The Four Madmen' inspires me—it calls for me to exert myself. I am all on the alert—already at the first glance I have seen where the flesh is to cling to its skeleton. The promise of colour and form and the rhythms excites me—it is what I have been waiting for so long" (Craig 1911, 165).

In 1901, when Craig staged *The Masque of Love* for the Purcell Opera Society, he had adapted Henry Purcell's music for Beaumont and Fletcher's drama *The Prophetess; or, The History of Dioclesian* into something like a scenario. In fact, in order to emphasize movement Craig cut out nearly sixty percent of the lyrics. This adaptation permitted wide range to his imagination, in the way a scenario permitted such range to the *commedia* actor. The connection to *commedia* is strong in *The Masque of Love,* for Craig used a simple platform stage and basic settings of curtains to feature a chorus of Pierrots as marionettes manipulated by another chorus made up of Harlequins. Stylized choreographic movements set to music accentuated the emotional content of the mythical love story. The result was that Craig tested many of his evolving theories while exploring the visual possibilities suggested by the freedom of *commedia*'s scenarios and the universality inherent in *commedia*'s stock characters.

Similarly important for modern *commedia* artists was their understanding that the popularity of *commedia* varied over the centuries as the forms and characters it inspired evolved, supplying diverse entertainments throughout Europe's theatres. At this point divergent notions of what *commedia* was, and what it could be, seem to emerge. Although some nineteenth-century artists were inspired by *commedia* characters and images (George Sand, for example, experimented with *commedia*-inspired improvisation in modest productions of Angelo Beolco's comedies at her Nohant Theatre in the late 1850s and early 1860s), at the beginnings of the twentieth century an astonishingly diverse group of playwrights, actors, directors, and designers in many cultures rediscovered the potency of *commedia* in ways that would permanently change the direction of the modern theatre. Craig, Luigi Pirandello, Vsevolod Meyerhold, Max Reinhardt, and Jacques Copeau, among many others, looked to *commedia* as they sought liberation from the pervasiveness of naturalism, as well as from the stale remnants of elaborate spectacles, melodramas, and played-out acting styles of the preceding century. Their unique ideas about its spirit and traditions permitted their rich imaginations wide scope as they attempted to define *commedia* and to apply their notions of it to plays and productions. Most of them viewed *commedia* as an amalgam of impulses and elements from traditional Italian improvised comedy, as well as its many antecedents and derivatives: classical comedy, medieval jesters and farces, the comedies of Molière, the Venetian plays of Goldoni, the *fiabe* of Gozzi, Pierrot in the tradition of Deburau, pantomimes, music hall, circus, carnival, street entertainments of all kinds, and the variety stage. Some common threads emerge: significantly, they rediscovered improvisation, masks, stereotypical characters, and an emphasis on the eloquence of physical movement through their understanding of *commedia*. They also noted the centrality of the *commedia* actor who, aided by stock masks and scenarios, could rise above realistic illusion to create universally recognized human symbols. The spontaneity of the improvisatory *commedia* style with its energy and direct assault on the senses of its audience had virtually no parallel in modern theatre. Another important idea was that a *commedia*-inspired theatre offered a style of ritualized carnival—a popular street theatre that served not only as communal fun, but also as a political instrument through its ever-present satire and mockery of the powerful. To fail to see *commedia* as inherently political is, I believe, to misunderstand its nature and its longevity.

This seemingly casual and lowly form of theatre became a *lingua franca* of the imagination, connecting cultures and artists throughout Europe, proving it could once again cross boundaries of culture and language in the twentieth century, as it had in the sixteenth and seventeenth centuries.

Despite their individual differences, modern *commedia* artists share the view that *commedia* is theatrical art at its pinnacle of expressiveness and creativity. Many of them were drawn toward a kind of archetypal Jungian vision that reduced and also transformed life into a handful of simple plots and stereotypical figures that confront us with spiritual and intellectual glimpses of our deepest beings. The characters of *commedia* thus became the expression of the universally human; to the modern mind, the characters' magic was powerful because it was a kind of street psychology. Particularly in the character of Arlecchino, modern theatre found a model in which to embody an absurdly lyrical vision of contemporary humanity, culminating in such creations as Charlie Chaplin's

"Little Tramp," Samuel Beckett's hobos, and Eugene Ionesco's existential clowns.

Martin Green and John Swan, authors of *The Triumph of Pierrot*, a chronicle of the cultural influence of *commedia* as exemplified by the figure of Pierrot, rightly explain that for twentieth-century artists *commedia* "is not an idea or a meaning, but a collection of images with many meanings" (1986, xiii). For some, such as Meyerhold, Dario Fo, and The San Francisco Mime Troupe, *commedia* offered a platform for counter-information and overt political statements. The San Francisco Mime Troupe and groups like El Teatro Campesino and The Bread and Puppet Theatre began using *commedia* techniques to develop an ensemble acting style suited to a radical theatre of the people. These groups create their performances in a communal way, with participants collaborating on the performance by working from a sketchy play, often resembling a *commedia* scenario, but with little real improvisation happening in front of the audience.

For other artists like Craig, Meyerhold, and Copeau, *commedia* provided techniques that helped them reconsider the techniques of acting and directing. For Copeau, the direct communication (and communion) with the audience and the universality of the *commedia* stock characters were the elements he wished to recover for the modern stage from *commedia* tradition. Copeau helped each of his actors to find a specific stock character directly inspired by *commedia* masks, with the intention that each actor would play a basic stereotype regardless of the particular play being produced. The actor could add elements of his own personality and other embellishments without undermining the simplicity and clarity of his or her stock character. These characters represented basic human behaviors (good and bad) and also suggested various classes and professions. It seemed to Copeau that such characters could serve, as they had originally in *commedia,* as human symbols playing out the ultimate comedy of life. Copeau's desire to re-theatricalize the theatre with the spirit and techniques of *commedia* led him to discard the literary texts of the plays and to turn them into rough scenarios. Contrary to what is often written, some of Copeau's most important *commedia* experiments were done later in his career, when he retreated to Burgundy with a young company *(les Copiaus)* in 1924. He adapted three traditional *commedia scenari,* all of which emphasized masks, movement, pantomime, and music, with a minimum of plot complexity or dialogue (*Harlequin the Magician* [1925], *The Illusion* [1926], and Beolco's *The Women of Ancona* [1927]). Mostly as a result of Copeau's influence on a generation of French actors that included Louis Jouvet, Charles Dullin, and Jean-Louis Barrault, *commedia* plays, productions, and performance techniques were commonplace in France and supplied a multitude of images for the plays of the Absurdists. The techniques of modern mime pioneered by Étienne Decroux and popularized by Jacques Lecoq and Marcel Marceau also owe much to *commedia*.

Some modern theatrical artists, like Reinhardt, were merely *commedia* antiquarians, reviving its buffoonery and spontaneity to delight modern audiences with its carnival spirit. Others, like Meyerhold and his contemporaries Alexander Tairov and Eugene Vakhtangov, and later, such contemporary directors as Peter Brook, Ariane Mnouchkine, Giorgio Strehler, and Eugenio Barba, broke free of the naturalistic stage to create various new kinds of production styles and techniques built, in part, on *commedia* traditions. Playwrights including Pirandello, Beckett, Ionesco, Eduardo de Filippo, Nikolai Evreinov, Bertolt Brecht, Hugo von Hofmannsthal, Paul Ernst, Stefan Zweig, a number of Spanish dramatists of the "Generation of '98," and, to a lesser degree, such English playwrights as Shaw, J. M. Barrie, and Harley Granville-Barker, found models for characters and situations in *commedia*'s scenarios and characters.

All of these artists quite obviously interpret *commedia* broadly and individually. Like the best and rarest forms of theatre, *commedia* was both spiritual and intellectual. It also proved to be universally malleable and national, adapting in each country where it appeared to the needs of that culture's artists and audiences.

During the last quarter of the twentieth century, *commedia* has clearly become a paradigm for theatre at the height of its expressive and technical powers; its echoes can be heard everywhere. The scenarios can still provide us with the inspiration to develop new strands of *commedia*-inspired theatre today, as Craig envisioned eighty years ago.

Works Cited

Craig, Edward Gordon. *Daybook II*. January 7, 1911.
———. "The *Commedia dell'Arte* Ascending." *The Mask*. 5:2 (1912): 104–108.
Green, Martin, and John Swan. *The Triumph of Pierrot*. New York: Macmillan, 1986.

Symposium Discussion

Edited by Paul C. Castagno

CASTAGNO: What is a scenario? This open-ended question has been the subject of an ongoing debate among Italian scholars of the *commedia dell'arte*. I would like to begin by considering Marotti's introduction to his transcribed text of the Scala *scenari*. In this introduction, Marotti explores a number of critical views and perceptions that will offer us a starting point, while familiarizing our larger audience with some of the Italian scholarship in this area. We can then progress toward Zorzi's structural scheme of the *canovaccio,* discuss it, and see how it works for us.

To begin, one series of comments in Marotti's introduction compared the scenario to a musical score: the notion of superimposed multiple lines, or how it's like a transcription/reduction of an orchestral score to the piano. Could we comment on these considerations? Is there any sense of their being valid?

HECK: I have never thought of it that way, because usually what you try to do with a piano reduction is still have a full impression of musical content from the beginning to the end of the piece. You drop texture, but you keep the same number of measures. As a result, you get a sense of the flow from beginning to end. But what happens in the scenario is that you create an "unfinished symphony." You drop measures, you sketch the beginning of the theme and let the performer—the actor—finish this melody; then you sketch another melody and let someone else finish it. So, I think that this analogy limps from my perspective.

CASTAGNO: So if we parallel a musical measure with a dramatic beat it should follow what Marotti says: that the extended comedy in all its beats would constitute the orchestral score.

HECK: Perhaps, yes, yes.

SWAN: But, Tom, in your presentation you talked about a guitar tablature . . .

HECK: Yes, I made a reference to a line with some chord symbols on it; no meter, no melody, nothing but harmony and chord strokes as the earliest guitar tablature that exists. That's the kind of notation from which we get the basic *ciaccona* structure and other chordal formulas. They start out as very, very sketchy in the sixteenth century, but by the time we are in the eighteenth century they are fully fleshed out in the hands of the more literate artists in central and northern Europe.

CASTAGNO: Perhaps a loose parallel can be drawn here to Goldoni or Marivaux, who made similar attempts during the eighteenth century—by fleshing out and taking the sketchy, and improvised *commedia* into a more literary realm.

SWAN: Yes.

CASTAGNO: Another thing that came up here is the notion of establishing a dominant tone: a scenario does not just represent a variety of actions; rather each scenario possesses a dominant tone. Did you find that true, especially in regard to the comedy, pastoral, and tragi-comedy that were read?

FISHER: Well, from the standpoint of an actor, each scenario seemed to have its own rhythm and tempo, to put it in as general a way as possible.

CASTAGNO: So perhaps we do have a pervasive or dominant tone, not one that was continually being undercut by the comic interplay, say, between Pantalone and Zanni, for instance.

SWAN: I have trouble with the notion of a dominant tone, particularly if you look at *The Madness of Isabella.* Isabella herself is a tragic figure. It's understood that she's been wronged and that she's mad. Well, now that she's mad, she can do this comic number. It doesn't mean that there isn't a dominant tone, but it means that it is very, very malleable; I think it goes back to Jim's point made earlier about remembering the performance-oriented nature of this *tirata* in a very specific way. There is no tone presented by the scenario that could not be overwhelmed by a forceful personality like Isabella's.

FISHER: Also, the nature of a main character at the center of a farce, no matter how amusing it is to the audience—that character is going through a tragedy. I think of Mel Brooks's comment that tragedy is when

I cut my finger, but comedy is when you fall into an open sewer and die. It's the perspective that all farces are a tragedy to the character at the center of the piece.

QUINN: I feel a little confused by the word tone, but what I think you're using here is a word for something like a literary effect—that as you read it some sort of mood or feeling comes through the text. That's a fine idea; I don't see any reason why that can't be true. We need to rethink the way literature relates to the theatre, generally. We have anxiety about the absence of scripted dialogue. It is the same anxiety that Goldoni had in 1742. We need to think about the way literature relates to the theatre in much broader terms, because people don't just produce plays, they produce lyric poems, they produce novels. You can read the *scenari* as literature if you like. It may not be good literature but maybe once in a while it is.

CASTAGNO: These comments can move us into something that seems to be in the air: that Flaminio Scala was really one of the first to point at the complexity of the problem, that is to say, the relation of the dramatic text to the performance text.

QUINN: Well, look at the way the *scenari* are laid out on the page. You get the argument, the characters, then the scenario, so that in a sense we get the story three times. We can imagine the argument and the characters as they fit into the scenario, and then it gets played out at greater length. So from this standpoint in a progression, the actual performance is only a fourth step, a final, more detailed playing through.

SWAN: There are some cases when the modernists play very knowingly with that disjunction. Meyerhold directed a production of a Molière play in which a character mouthed his lines, while at the same time mugged in such a way as to undercut everything he was saying—it was specifically designed that he do that. Again, in *The Madness of Isabella*, it becomes a semiotic question: what does the audience expect? They see this virtuosic actress, Isabella Andreini, coming on stage. They already expect something other than a realistic portrayal of a suffering woman. There is already an agreement with the audience, so you go to your system of signs, which is ripe for the undercutting of the scenario.

FISHER: It makes me think of the recent San Francisco Mime Troupe production of *Uncle Tom's Cabin*, which stripped away most of the play, keeping only the essences of the characters and situations. The performers argued, stepped outside of the play, and at one point dragged the author on stage, to berate her for the way she portrayed characters in that scene. This was a complete argument between the text and what the actors were doing with it.

CASTAGNO: So the implication here is that a dialectical *and very vital* relationship may be established, not only between the scenario and the performance text, but also between elements of the scenario, as Mike described.

FISHER: In the live performance, these dynamic tensions can be played out.

CASTAGNO: You know, on the other hand, one commentator in the Marotti text posited that the *scenari* proceed as cold, mute, dead cadavers in their naked schematization—which is a whole different take on the subject.

D'ANTUONO: I have a difficult time reading them as cold and dead. Maybe it is what the audience brings, that symbiotic relationship between the *commedia dell'arte* artist and the audience; that is, I'm bringing something to it that I think should be there. When I read it from my own background it comes alive for me.

CASTAGNO: Ludovico Zorzi said though for the nontheatrically astute reader it's already dead in the water. How many of you have the *scenari* as subject matter in your curriculum? It's not something that's studied very much. As a matter of fact, Zorzi talks about the students being bored by the bare bones of it all. They lack the patience that one has to have to get through the *scenari*.

AUDIENCE: That's their reaction to reading plays in general.

D'ANTUONO: That's their reaction to most literature.

SWAN: The scenario really does invite that reaction though, because it presents this outlandish sequence—and then that and then this—and if you have to read twenty of them at once, you climb the walls.

FISHER: It's a blueprint, not a play.

SWAN: Yes, it's not Boccaccio, in other words.

AUDIENCE: When I introduce the scenario to theatre history students, their first question is usually "What is this supposed to look like?" Once you establish what this is, everything else fills in. When I say, "We are going to read a play today," that serves as a symbol for them; they understand on a literary level and can see all the possibilities.

Once they understand what the other elements are within the whole context of *commedia dell'arte*, that scenario does become something concrete. I relate the same way you do, Nancy; I see so many other possibilities once I start reading through it.

QUINN: There are a couple of people in semiotics who try to deal with texts that way. Anne Ubersfeld talks about texts being full of holes, and then this whole process of filling any text in—especially a play text. She calls it "concretization," a term she borrows from Roman Ingarden.

CASTAGNO: Iser talks about the same phenomenon in *Act of Reading*, this notion of concretization, of filling gaps. With the *scenari,* the reader really has to build the text, actually construct the imagery of action.

AUDIENCE: Right. Exactly. Generally, what happens with students of theatre very early is, at some point, they see imagery in a play. And so when I say "play," they say, "Ah! I have an image of what this could be about." It gets very difficult to feel a sense of life in a play, until you have some kind of concrete reference that fills in the whole picture.

QUINN: Yes, a philosopher who has done the most sustained work in this kind of text is Nelson Goodman in *Languages of Art.* He talks about things like notation scores and musical scores as intermediate forms, which preserve these images within them, but are also meant to be evocative. They aren't the complete artwork and they aren't meant to be read for pleasure or entertainment, although I suppose there are people who can read a score and get great pleasure from it, but not many, and not all the time.

CASTAGNO: This whole question of the *scenari* as a notational score, or as an intermediate form raises an interesting conundrum regarding the identification of the *scenari* as texts. Do the *scenari* serve as *a priori* guides to performance, or were they written after the fact—a record, a representation of a fossil, of a lost spectacle?

QUINN: I don't know. You can read this history many different ways, and there are people here who know more about this than I do. One thing that you have to keep in mind is that in a print culture, to print something is to claim it for your own somehow, and to establish a kind of legitimacy for it that justifies the expense of the gesture of printing. So we have to assume that something in the history of Scala's company led him to this venture.

CASTAGNO: Yes, well there was the idea of raising the status of the Confidenti, which he led as *capocomico,* to the stature of the Gelosi. Publication provided this link, through the network of associations, if nothing else. By publishing this collection, Scala positioned himself as a major protagonist in the history of *commedia*—he immortalized its golden age.

The Scala *scenari* in actuality provide *the* model of the *commedia dell'arte* as Bartoli tells us. Both Sanesi and Apollonio would agree and have referred to it as "the academic canon of the improvised." On the other hand, Scala, who was a tailor by trade, and getting on in years, probably wanted to capitalize in some way on its publication.

QUINN: If they are so widely known and disseminated that they had no more value as secret plans, then the point would be to make them public plans to return something on the investment that way.

HECK: Something else about the issue of the scenario and its nature: let's not forget that, for the public, the scenario was not an issue, because they never saw it. For the public it was the actual performance that was the issue. There is a very telling line in the Giovan Andreini text, *Le due commedie in commedia*. There is a conversation between Calandra, Lelio, and Filino. Lelio, referring to a person who was just speaking, says that he was singing in an improvised way. But Calandra says, *"e cosa pensata questa, e non improvvisa"* ("it was something that I thought, it was not improvised"). But he goes on to say, *"ma non si può dire"* ("but you really can't tell"). You can't tell whether I had thought about it, or I had improvised it. Filino agrees: *"Oh no certo"* ("oh you sure can't"). You see, you can't tell as a member of the audience when there's a good play that comes on, whether those guys memorize their lines from a text or work them out in an improvised way. If it's well done you just can't tell the difference . . . well, almost.

FISHER: I do think that the *scenari* have been dangerous in a way; that is, people look at them sometimes as a capturing of *commedia dell'arte*, and they think: "That alone is what it was," and they don't see anything else in it. I do think that's a problem.

SWAN: Paul's point about fossilization I think still holds. Look for instance at Andreini's *bravure*—his creation of the remarkable Captain Spavento. But then he soon entered literature, leaving theatre. The *commedia* characters are indeed fossils, and by entering literature, they also changed the semiotic system.

FISHER: I think it destroys *commedia*'s reputation. People cannot understand what *commedia* was, because they look at the *scenari* and say, "That's it?"

SWAN: Ironically, *commedia* elevated its reputation by making itself literary, but at the same time betrayed it.

CASTAGNO: Yet in another sense, synchronically speaking, Scala's *scenari* provided a needed vindication or defense of the comic profession solely in artistic terms. It was, as Marotti states, devised to achieve a rapprochement between the literary and the comic. The contrast was to the more or less polemical treatises and defenses of Cecchini (Fritellino) and Barbieri (Beltrame), which were targeted, in the main, at the authorities of the Counter Reformation, who had made no distinctions at all between the professional *comici* and the charlatans.

QUINN: I guess this is where these other kinds of records really become crucial, so that instead of just resting with the *scenari,* you begin to look at some of the things that will allow you to reconstruct other things about the performance.

FISHER: Iconography.

QUINN: Yes.

AUDIENCE: It is interesting to look at this problem in relation to film studies. Film studies as a discipline got started before a lot of screenplays were reprinted. Now, screenplays are a part of film studies, but nobody looks at a screenplay and says, "That's the movie!" In fact, some of the first screenplays that were sold in the bookstores were Kaufman's *A Night at the Opera* and *A Day at the Races.* These were printed in a double volume that contained the "pre-shoot" screenplay followed by a transcription of what was actually seen on the screen. In the former there are stage directions such as "Harpo enters," and two pages later, "Harpo exits." There is nothing in the screenplay about what he does. One way to clarify the relationship of the *scenari* to a performance is to make that analogy and say, "Look at the screenplay and then look at the film."

CASTAGNO: Zorzi moves a step beyond what you're talking about—the notion of the text and its subsequent representation—by taking an X-ray view of a typical scenario (see graph). Zorzi offers us a metastructural scheme that illustrates the interactive connections between characters, what he describes as the "structural base of the scenario" *(struttura-base del canovaccio).* This scheme opens up all kinds of possibilities that one can detect. What are our reactions to Zorzi's diagram? Is this something that is sound, or applicable? Zorzi suggested that the *scenari* his students transcribed follow these formats as well.

QUINN: Could you explain what that means, Paul? To me looking at that, I don't understand the point of the lines.

CASTAGNO: Please refer to the captions under the graphic, which I've translated from Zorzi's statements in his article *Intorno alla commedia dell'arte* (Zorzi 1980, 433–35). Note that Zorzi uses the term "vectors" instead of lines, in order to imply a clear sense of magnitude or force, as well as direction.

AUDIENCE: One way to look at the lines is as indicators of relationships of dependency between the characters. It is impossible to sum up all possible relationships.

D'ANTUONO: So it is dependency.

AUDIENCE: Yes. Whether it is economic or sexual or . . .

CASTAGNO: It shows the sociocultural hierarchy from the subordinate characters to the more powerful characters at the top. It also gives us a sense of the hegemonic relations.

AUDIENCE: All plot summaries can be reduced to twenty or thirty types, so it represents a static form.

HECK: It's of limited use. I've seen this called a "sociogram." Sociologists use it to show how people interact with their friends.

QUINN: This seems to me to be the mistake of a graph like this one. It is all very neat and wonderfully laid out. It's a very pretty graph. But it overlooks the structural aspect of the plays that Chomsky would probably call generative. There is no limit to the number of times, or order, in which these things can happen, or to the extent in which they can occur. Once you approach the *scenari* as Zorzi has, you move from something like 36 situations to 2,000 dramatic situations. The range of complexity may as well be infinite. If he is tired of the whole system, he has my sympathy, but it isn't because it lacks possibilities for combination.

CASTAGNO: Zorzi does in fact acknowledge this potential for elaboration and variation and admits to its possibly damaging effects on his scheme. But he does suggest, in another vein, that this scheme functions in what you could call a "generative" sense—applying it as the basis of several other theatrical forms: from the antique Roman comedies, to Goldoni's *commedie regolari,* to the opera, among others.

AUDIENCE: Well, of course, many of the basic plots from those theatrical forms are similar. In fact, it sometimes seems that the plots of the *commedia* are infinite variations of the same story.

D'ANTUONO: That's the criticism of the Spanish Golden Age plays; it's the same plot over and over again. You don't have in the Spanish Golden

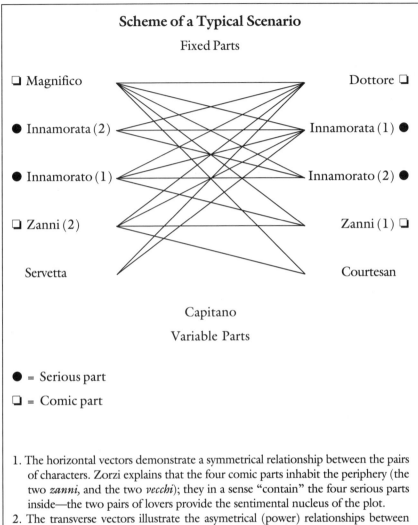

Scheme of a Typical Scenario

Fixed Parts

❏ Magnifico   Dottore ❏

● Innamorata (2)   Innamorata (1) ●

● Innamorato (1)   Innamorato (2) ●

❏ Zanni (2)   Zanni (1) ❏

Servetta   Courtesan

Capitano

Variable Parts

● = Serious part

❏ = Comic part

1. The horizontal vectors demonstrate a symmetrical relationship between the pairs of characters. Zorzi explains that the four comic parts inhabit the periphery (the two *zanni,* and the two *vecchi*); they in a sense "contain" the four serious parts inside—the two pairs of lovers provide the sentimental nucleus of the plot.
2. The transverse vectors illustrate the asymetrical (power) relationships between individual characters (for example, the parental relationship between father and son), or they indicate social, economic and even sexual dependence in regard to role (for example, the courtesan and a *zanni* who functioned as her pimp).

Age an *Othello* that stands out or a *Hamlet*. Who remembers the names of any of the heroes? They are all Don something or other. It's the same combination over and over of the same basic plot elements; yes, even the Spanish *comedia* . . .

HECK: Could I make an interdisciplinary remark in that regard? Let's not expect too much, folks, of theatre, considering that it has been said that Vivaldi didn't write five hundred *concerti*, he wrote one *concerto* five hundred times.

D'ANTUONO: Yes, but that gave us five hundred listening pleasures.

HECK: Well, the point is that you could also remonstrate with Renaissance architects for building one building forty times. Let's admit that within the frameworks that exist, you make your art.

SWAN: As I understand it that's not the parallel. The parallel really is to go back to Northrup Frye. You are looking for some basic typologies, and Luigi Dallapiccola's canard about Vivaldi was designed to say there was only one *concerto*, literally.

HECK: But that's stupid.

SWAN: It is indeed stupid!

AUDIENCE: With all respect to the *commedia*, when you begin to see the *commedia* in everything, you have the same problem with certain types of mythologists who identify mythic patterns and see them everywhere. So you say, "OK, there is the same mythic pattern in every country in the world." Either you are stuck trying to see how each country uses it differently, or else you try to trace it back to one coordinate.

CASTAGNO: Yes, well it was Apollonio who did just that with regard to the *commedia dell'arte*, when he said that the basic structural unit of *commedia* was the Pantalone/Zanni exchange.

HECK: The master/servant thing.

CASTAGNO: Which breaks down into even more distillation than we just saw with the Zorzi scheme.

HECK: I think they got cynical because they worked on it too long.

SWAN: You're taking on the whole structural enterprise. I do think we really can learn a lot from the four types of Northrup Frye. All of imaginative literature, including drama, including *commedia*, disappears into that structure in a very interesting way. It isn't reductive.

CASTAGNO: But then there's this sense of *commedia* as a mixture or even contamination of theatrical sources that makes genre-building problematic.

D'ANTUONO: Yes, we could consider the mixing of cultural sources as well. It's not a pure thing at all.

CASTAGNO: Let's move on to some other concerns. Are the *scenari* too removed from contemporary culture to be of any use?

D'ANTUONO: I think they would be very effective if you divided a class into four groups of students, gave each group the same basic plot, and said, "Think it all out and then present it on stage with no text. Just think about it and create the roles that you want to play." You'd get four different variations and thereby make your point.

AUDIENCE: And then you might not.

D'ANTUONO: Well, you're bound to get at least two versions. You don't find that much commonality among students.

QUINN: Only from the perspective which proposes that all plays are designed to instruct and to provide models for behavior. Obviously, in contemporary America, we would not want to promote the resolution of these plays into a comfortable patriarchal marriage.

Nor would we need to bring to the theatre the notion that we should present only things that we approve. One of the fundamental principles of comedy is, that you laugh at the mistakes that people make. Over a three-hundred-year tradition, these comedies provide infinite examples of how foolish fathers can be. So, the relation of these plays to the contemporary political moment is extremely complicated. If you were to write them up, you could make some sort of bizarre historical rule out of the situation of the *scenari*, like how female desire leads the play through its motion.

FISHER: You are on tricky ground though when you eliminate the idea that comedy serves as a corrective. Molière commented that comedy exists to show a man his vices and then to show him how to correct them. That connects it immediately to the political aspects of *commedia*.

QUINN: But it's up then to the audience to decide these things. He leaves us at the end of *The Misanthrope* with an extremely ambivalent situation, and I think you can do the same thing with a *commedia dell'arte* scenario.

CASTAGNO: We find this sense of ambivalence when we move into the realm of iconography. For instance, in the early iconography of the *com-*

media you just get the grotesque and the erotic—with no denunciations underneath, no caption saying that this is the wrong way to live. Late in the cinquecento—in part as a result of the religious reforms, particularly in the North—various mottoes appear, which warn the viewer against what is pictured in the image.

QUINN: Yes, so it requires an understanding of what is not to be done in order to avoid it.

CASTAGNO: But the question of moral intent is difficult to assess. Some artists were perhaps simply trying to appease the authorities; others, the Flemish mostly, were schooled in the *vanitas* tradition.

SWAN: It's not just the moral scheme that applies here. This idea may be hopeless and "influence heavy," but I still think there is something about the energy of a scenario that parallels a number of very well constructed farce films. My favorite modern example, because it does end in this kind of resolution you are talking about, is Danny DeVito in *Ruthless People*. There is something fulfilling about its tightly constructed action. It is similar to the pattern of energy in the *scenari*, which played itself out with the moral resolutions clearly in the background.

QUINN: One of the most interesting things happening in contemporary Italian semiotics is related not only to this iconographic question that Paul brought up, but also to this question of energy. A couple of people have been working with Eugenio Barba on this notion of pre-performance gestures, which were written or drawn into some of the *commedia* gestures. The characters not only had psychic attitudes like hunger and desire, but also had physical attitudes that exemplified them. Unfortunately, we can't get these too clearly from the scenarios, but from the iconographic sources. Some of Watteau's paintings use these gestures out of context, in order to recreate an imaginary history. You get a record of something that is happening in the body as it prepares to act. It is still semiotics somehow, but it is an entrance into the system, it is the gesture of taking off on this whole code of behavior.

D'ANTUONO: It's like reading an opera aria, reading the music, and then watching an artist perform it. The nuances that the artist brings may not be in the written text. You get the notes, but not the interpretations. So, you are looking at music that appears very nice, and you can imagine what it must sound like. But without the artist's performance, you miss a dimension. That's why you have to be careful with the *scenari* not to say, "That's all there is." Well, that's not all there is. You may have to intuit it to fill it in.

CASTAGNO: Perhaps these considerations—that there is something more, that *commedia* has so many dimensions—can bring us to our final question. What future research or directions are indicated in the area of *commedia dell'arte?*

HECK: Let's broaden the question to ask that, if we don't have anything specific we want people to run out and do, we might report on what is being done right now that sounds interesting. What's happening in *commedia* just from our perspectives?

SWAN: In the music aspect, a graduate student in New York is exploring the commonalities and the strategies in the twentieth-century *"commedia"* music of the composers Strauss and Busoni. Indeed, this is an area that is underexplored, like so many—think of all the untranslated *scenari*.

FISHER: John Swan's and Martin Green's book *The Triumph of Pierrot* seems to open up entirely the field of the influence of *commedia* on the arts of the twentieth century. Take *commedia* ballet—nobody's touched it. There's a lot there just waiting for somebody to look into it.

HECK: From my point of view, what needs to be done is a serious look at bringing out an edition of the sources of the *scenari*—those various collections of *scenari* that were once transcribed by the students of Zorzi, but have never been published. Someone in America may do it first, because I believe the Italians with whom I've had contact, much as I respect them as individual scholars, don't seem to have enough desire to get together and do it; or they are waiting for funding or something. But I suspect that by the year 2000, we will have a good diplomatic transcription of all these *scenari* sources in Italian and possibly in English, as well. I personally am interested in the Warsaw/Dresden group and have ordered microfilm at this point. I've never actually seen them before.

In my own research, my next step will probably be to complete a proper musical iconography of the *commedia dell'arte*, something that could be published. I do have a slide show on this subject, but to get it from that state to a fully documented textual form will take a couple of years.

QUINN: There are a couple of things happening now in America that people should know about. Virginia Scott is following up her book on the seventeenth-century French/Italian *commedia* with an eighteenth-century book, which I think will be a collection of essays. It is much more difficult to do a systematic treatment of the eighteenth century. The other person who is preparing a major book is Anya Peterson-Royce. That should be forthcoming soon, because she has published a couple of preliminary essays, and some journal articles take a long time to come out.

As for my own preferences, I would like a little bit more interdisciplinary research, particularly in the way people look at iconographic sources for evidence. I think the kinds of evidence that people have looked for have been narrowly conceived in some cases. Paintings are looked at for specific attributes and figures, or possibilities of relations to plays, rather than looked at gesturally as part of cultural systems of meaning, so that the sorts of systems are much more complicated and interconnected than people have come to terms with. That area seems to me to be one of the possibilities that semiotics offers for further research: a greater emphasis on a whole cultural system rather than a distinct set of modern disciplines that we are trying to retrace into a culture that didn't have them.

CASTAGNO: Michael refers in part to what I am trying to do with my article on the grotesque in early *commedia dell'arte* iconography, which was published in the 1992 annual of *Theatre History Studies*. This grotesque reading of *commedia* figures attempts to signify or illuminate these subversive images within the sociocultural *carnevale* context of late sixteenth-century Europe. On a larger scale, my forthcoming book, *The Early* Commedia dell'Arte *(1550–1621): The Mannerist Context* (Peter Lang, 1993) identifies the early *commedia dell'arte*—in particular, the iconography—as a Mannerist phenomenon. Thus, the synchronic links to this pervasive international style of art in the cinquecento will attempt to establish the *commedia* aesthetic as Mannerist, rather than as a product of the Renaissance, which has been the case up to now. It's actually a very conservative premise because the artistic and cultural factors are so closely linked. Some of these principles are evidenced in what Stan Longman shows us at the Sabbioneta Court Theatre (see below, p. 59): the *trompe l'oeil* fresco of a Pantalone, whereby the painting competed with and commented on the live performance; where there were multiple points-of-view, and visual puns. And this same thing happened at Trausnitz where the frescoes of *commedia* figures seemed to play against the actual architecture of the hall; where the *trompe l'oeil* figures seem actually to jump out at you from the walls. It was a mesh, because Mannerism brought theatricality to art, and *commedia* brought theatricality to the stage.

I also explore the aesthetic principles of *maniera* and suggest a number of ways in which those principles might be applied to the *commedia dell'arte*. For instance, take *Innocence Restored*, which had myriad versions of the same basic story. It is similar to what the *maniera* artists did. They had the same basic composition, or put together parts of several compositions, and it was always their virtuosity that they brought forth. They focused on the expression of the idea, rather than the original idea itself.

I should mention that Renzo Guardenti, whom I met while doing research in Florence, has completed a comprehensive study of *commedia* iconography in seventeenth-century France.

D'ANTUONO: I think I'm the only one doing what I'm doing. I have transcribed about thirty of the *scenari*. I have to transcribe them because I can't read or work with them unless I write them out in Italian—the chicken scratches defy description. I sit there with a magnifying glass trying to decide if this letter is an "l" or a "t," and how to read that "l" or "t" or whatever it is. What would I be interested in? If I live long enough to do it all, it will be out in ten years.

CASTAGNO: Amen!

Work Cited

Zorzi, Ludovico. "Intorno alla Commedia dell'Arte: Due Lezioni." *Forum Italicum*. 14:2 (1980): 426–53.

Part II

A Renaissance Anomaly

A *Commedia dell'Arte* Troupe in Residence at the Court Theatre at Sabbioneta

Stanley V. Longman

THE EARLIEST documentary evidence of a troupe of *commedia dell'arte* players dates from February 25, 1545, when eight players met in Padua to form the "fraternal company" of Ser Maphio. The same year marked the beginning of the Council of Trent, resulting in the Counter-Reformation. In the spirit of that movement, many attacks were launched against professional players. These include, among others, the severe strictures issued by Carlo Borromeo, Cardinal and Archbishop of Milan from 1560 until his death in 1584, the suppression of the *commedia* in Rome under Popes Gregory XIII and Clement VIII, and what was perhaps the most vitriolic and influential of the polemics, *Della Christiana moderatione del theatro* (On Christian Moderation of the Theatre) published in 1652 by Father Giulio Domenico Ottonelli. From 1545 to well into the seventeenth century, *commedia* players fought to establish their art as a distinct and honorable profession. Modern scholars, including Luciano Mariti and Ferdinando Taviani, argue that the *commedia*'s greatest contribution was to turn theatre into an institution with a place of its own in society. Vespasiano Gonzaga, Duke of Sabbioneta, offered an early but short-lived alternative to theatrical vagabondage when he built his court theatre and invited a company of *commedia* players to take up residence there.

Theatre generally was regarded as a variety of festivity; Mariti argues, "Baroque society lacked any clear definition of the role of theatre in society and treated it and the art of acting ambiguously" (1980, 62). Performance was among the ephemera of carnival, royal entries, courtly marriage celebrations—and now increasingly of mountebank acts in the piazzas. At court, players were servants hired to provide entertainment on special occasions and festivals. Having fulfilled their obligation, the players would take to the road again hoping that the duke of the next city would grant permission to perform in his city streets and squares.[1] Florence had the strange arrangement of the Teatro di Baldracca, located in one of the city's "districts of ill repute" (Carrandini 1990, 129), and yet adjacent to the east wing of the Uffizi Palace. *Commedia* performances were staged there as early as 1576 for the populace with the special provision of "stanzini," or little rooms, some with grating across the front for privacy. From one of these, accessible through a hidden passageway, the Grandduke of Tuscany and his family could watch the show unobserved (Zorzi 1980, 355–56. Cf. Evangelista 1979). On another occasion, the same *commedia* company might present a command performance for the Grandduke next door in the Uffizi.

In the midst of this unsettling ambiguity, for a very brief period, one company of *commedia* players was blessed with its own specially constructed court theatre. That theatre is the "Teatro all'Antica" (Theatre in the Ancient Manner), built in 1588 for the court of Duke Vespasiano Gonzaga of Sabbioneta, a theatre that still exists. It was inaugurated during carnival in 1590, when three amateur groups and a professional company performed there. The Duke took such delight in these performances that he conceived the idea of a resident *commedia* company for his new theatre. He ordered such a company formed, and it arrived in late April and spent a twenty-day sojourn at court. That appears to have been the first and last residency of the Duke's company. They may have returned in September, but no record exists. By carnival the next year, the Duke was gravely ill. He died February 27, 1591, putting an end to this unique arrangement of a resident *commedia* company at court. But in that brief period, three weeks in late April and May 1590, the Duke provided a stability and dignity for a *commedia dell'arte* company unheard of in its time.

The theatre building itself is unique: it was the first theatre in Italy since Roman times to be built from the ground up as a permanent theatre. All the previous theatres, including the famous Teatro Olimpico of 1585 in Vicenza, were constructed within existing structures or were intended only as temporary structures—such as the Campidoglio Theatre built in Rome in 1513. Commonly, a platform stage and stands for the audience would be erected in a large hall and easily disassembled to restore the hall to its previous configuration once the festival had passed.

---

[1]An enlightening account of the players' search for performance space is found in Anderson 1988.

Vespasiano Gonzaga, however, wanted a permanent theatre. He himself had undertaken the urban planning of Sabbioneta, hoping to give it the appearance of an ideal city-state. He laid out a careful network of streets and quarters within the city walls of Sabbioneta and provided new structures for all important civic and religious functions: the ducal governmental palace, the ducal residential palace, the Garden House, the Church of the Incoronata, a synagogue, a school, a mint, an armory, a printing press, and finally, as the crowning glory, a theatre.

In May 1588, the Duke commissioned Vincenzo Scamozzi to design and build a theatre. Just three years earlier, Scamozzi had completed the Teatro Olimpico begun by Andrea Palladio in Vicenza. Unlike the Olimpico, which was an academy theatre dedicated to the performance of tragedy, or the later Teatro Farnese in Parma, which was a court theatre dedicated to the performance of courtly *intermezzi*, the Sabbioneta theatre was designed as a theatre for comedy. Scamozzi provided it with a Serlian comic scene, a perspective vista of private dwellings merging with frescoed towers and hills on the back walls. The theatre house contains three levels of mannerist commentary on the theatrical experience: across the top of the colonnade that surmounts the *cavea* are statues of the Olympian gods (from whom the theatre takes its alternate name of Teatro Olimpico). On the walls between the *cavea* and the stage are images of ancient Rome as the ideal city, reflected as well in the busts of various Roman emperors. Across the upper portions of the walls and at the edge of the stage are frescoes of windows and balustrades from which common people watch the action on stage. Indeed, one of those peering down on the stage is clearly Pantalone himself.

Thus, the theatre made comments on civic life on several levels: the "city" of the gods, the ideal city (ancient Rome), the vernacular city of the frescoed onlookers, and the comic city of the stage itself. All this, of course, is set within the emerging ideal city-state of Sabbioneta. The theatre is a city within a city within a city within a city. The idea of the city suits not only Vespasiano's pretensions toward a new Rome but also the spirit of comedy, a form of drama that tends to move toward a social bonding of its characters with the audience.[2]

Vincenzo Scamozzi came to Sabbioneta in May 1588 to survey the site for the theatre and to draw up the initial architectural plans. The building was completed and Scamozzi's comic scene installed by February 1590 when the theatre was inaugurated with performances that accompanied other carnival festivities (Mazzoni 1985, 87). Unfortunately, the scenery has disappeared, destroyed some time during the

---

[2]On the relation of city to theatre, see Zorzi 1977.

eighteenth century; nevertheless, Scamozzi's drawings for the comic scene have been preserved at the Uffizi in Florence. It would appear that the idea of dedicating the theatre to comedy had been an early decision. It is less certain when the Duke may have decided to make it the resident theatre of a *commedia* troupe. He must have done so some time shortly before or after carnival in 1590, to judge by extant contemporary accounts of the festivities.

One of these accounts appears in the extracts of the diary kept by a certain Nicolò de' Dondi, published much later (in 1857) under the title *Estratti del Diario delle cose avvenute in Sabbioneta dal MDLXXX al MDC* (Extracts of the Diary of Things Happening in Sabbioneta from 1580 to 1600). De' Dondi was present throughout the fifteen days of carnival festivities in 1590. The Duke held balls in the Salon di Cavalli, the "hall of horses," so named for the many equestrian statues of the Gonzagas displayed there. He entertained his son-in-law, the Prince of Stigliano, and Signor Giulio Cesare da Pomponesco and their retinues. De' Dondi's description reads in part:

> There was then also a company of players. When the day's festivities were concluded, they performed each evening either comedies or pastorals. And even during the day, when it was appropriate during carnival, the players performed in the Salon di Cavalli in the Palace as had been done before and another company of local players performed after supper, so we had two comedies a day. The local players made up three companies, one of young people from Sabbioneta, another from Bozzolo and still another from Guastalla. They performed on the new stage just completed for that purpose. They also tilted for the ring and planned to tilt at quintaine, but the bad weather prevented that. The previously mentioned company of players and the Duke concluded a yearly agreement whereby the company was obliged to perform in Sabbioneta two months out of every year, that is for fifteen days following Easter, another fifteen days at the Ascension of the Madonna in August, and a month at carnival time, while the Duke promised to pay them 400 scudi a year plus expenses during the two month residency. Moreover, the Duke had them take the name of the Confidenti and ordered them to bear his coat of arms and display it on the curtains wherever they performed to show that they were the players of the illustrious Duke of Sabbioneta. (De' Dondi 1857, 359–60)

This somewhat confused account does at least provide us with the most salient facts of the first use made of the Teatro all'Antica at Sabbioneta. It appears that in the last week of the carnival season, a company of professional *commedia* players joined three amateur, local companies to provide at least two plays a day. One of these took place in the daytime in the Salon di Cavalli and the other in the newly inaugurated theatre at night, using Scamozzi's suggestive lighting (Mazzoni and Guaita 1985, 88). De' Dondi is correct that the Duke issued an order for a company of players to become Players of the Duke in residence at his theatre two months out of every year. But it does not appear to have been exactly the same company that performed there for carnival in 1590, nor did the new company take the name "Confidenti." This company actually may have been the beginning of the famous Accesi Company, as we shall see.

A second contemporary document helps to resolve some of this confusion. It is the letter issued by the Duke Vespasiano Gonzaga through his secretary on March 18, 1590, ordering an actor named Silvio de' Gambi to organize a company in the Duke's name:

> Having built a theatre in this our city of Sabbioneda [*sic*] and desiring that it not remain empty, we shall have plays presented there at certain times of the year and we shall have a company of players under our name, and we order you, Messer Silvio de' Gambi of Ferrara, to assemble an honest company. To that purpose, we order you to travel to Mantua, Ferrara and wherever necessary to find the actors who may play the characters needed for this company. We pledge ourselves to pay for their residency the sum of 400 scudi per year, according to this agreement: they are to serve here two months out of the year, that is for twenty days during carnival time, twenty more after Easter, and twenty more in September, which amounts to a total of two months. For the remainder of the year they shall be free to go where they please as players retained by ourselves; and we promise as well to provide them with room and board during their residency. As a sign of our good faith, we have issued the present order and signed it with our own hand and affixed our seal, given in Sabbioneda in the Ducal Palace this 18th day of March 1590 (L.S.) Vespasiano Gonzaga Colonna, Paolo Emilio Liscati, Ducal Secretary. (Quoted in Mazzoni and Guaita 1985, 88–89)

This letter, carrying somewhat more weight than de' Dondi's observations, indicates that the professional company that performed at Sabbioneta for the inauguration of the theatre was not the company that became the Duke's Company. That company could not have come into existence until after the Duke's March 18 letter. The distribution of dates also does not quite square with de' Dondi's account, but at any rate both agree on a total of two months' residency. De' Dondi's mention of the title "Confidenti" is genuinely confusing. The Gonzagas of Mantua were patrons of the famous Confidenti Company, which had been in existence from 1580 forward. The Duke's new company has no recorded name, but there is some strong suggestion that it may have been the Accesi Company, which dates its origin from 1590 and became one of the leading *commedia* troupes of the seventeenth century under the leadership of Pier Maria Cecchini.

De' Gambi apparently went to work with considerable dispatch. De' Dondi confirms in his diary that the company came to Sabbioneta after Easter, as called for in the letter, and he himself saw them perform in the theatre on May 3, 1590, in a special presentation honoring the Marquis del Guasto (De' Dondi 1857, 361–62). This is de' Dondi's last mention of the company, suggesting that the planned return in September did not happen. By carnival, 1591, the Duke was gravely ill, and the company certainly did not return then. Thus the court theatre at Sabbioneta had a very brief life as a resident *commedia* theatre: perhaps twenty days in late April and early May 1590. Indeed, the theatre had a very brief life as a theatre: Inaugurated in February 1590, it fell into disuse immediately following the Duke's death. During a plague in 1629–30, it was used as an infirmary with its walls whitewashed. Later in the century it became a granary. It had brief revivals in the eighteenth century (when the scenery was removed) and again in the early nineteenth. When Gordon Craig visited the theatre in the 1920s, it had become a badly maintained movie house, its walls still whitewashed (Craig [1925] 1967, 132–33).

The company which de' Gambi put together may have had a happier fate. The connection with the Accesi is not absolutely clear. It is supported by a letter sent June 7, 1590, on behalf of Alfonso II d'Este, Duke of Ferrara, to the Governor of Modena: "His Highness the Duke has ordered me to write to Your Excellency to request that you receive the Duke of Sabbioneda's Company of Players (in which appears the character of Frittellino) in your city to perform plays during the present season for however long a period is mutually satisfactory. In closing, I kiss Your Excellency's hand and wish God grant you every happiness. In Ferrara this 7th day of June 1590, Your devoted servant, Giovan Battista Laderchi" (Solerti 1900, cviii; the letter is in the Archivio di Stato of Modena). The mention of Frittellino is particularly intriguing here. That mask was the exclusive property of Pier Maria Cecchini, a citizen of Ferrara and an actor who had performed at Mantua for the Duke Guglielmo Gonzaga from 1583 onward, according to one of Cecchini's own letters dated 1622 (Morinello 1955, 3:304). He took the name Frittellino (or "Little Fritter") from a jester in the Gonzaga court at the time of Gianfranco Gonzaga and Isabella d'Este. By all accounts he established his Accesi Company in 1590. There is another contemporary reference that suggests a connection: it is a record of a company lodged at the Albergo della Fortuna in Mantua on February 6, 1591, just at the time when Duke Vespasiano had taken ill. The record indicates that it was a company of *comici ferraresi* (players from Ferrara), and it lists among their members a certain "P. M. Chezzini," who almost certainly must have been Pier Maria Cecchini, and Gabriele Canovaro and Giovan Battista Austoni, both of whom were members of the Accesi (Cf. D'Ancona [1891] 1971, 2:502 and Molinari 1983, 16). This company may well have been the very one put together by Silvio de' Gambi about whom we know absolutely nothing.

Pier Maria Cecchini, however, was to emerge as one of the most prominent *commedia* players. His role, Frittellino, was a *zanni*. His wife Orsola, daughter of Flaminio Scala of the Gelosi Company, took the role of Flaminia, an *innamorata*. His company, the Accesi, performed throughout Italy: in Turin, Milan, Parma, Modena, Bologna, Padua, Venice, Florence, and Naples. According to Alessandro d'Ancona, the first record of the Accesi Company dates from January 1590, when it requested permission to perform at Brescia, after which there is no further record of the company until 1597 when it spent three months performing in Genoa (D'Ancona [1891] 1971, 2:495–96. Cf. Sanesi 1935, 2: 19–20). The company performed in France on a number of occasions: in Lyons in 1600 for the marriage of Maria de' Medici and King Henri IV, in Paris and Fontainebleau for the court from January to October 1601, and again from February to October 1608. It traveled to Austria in 1613 and 1614, where Cecchini so pleased the Emperor Matthias that he was rewarded with a knighthood. The company continued to perform until 1628.

During this time Cecchini became one of the most impassioned champions of the cause of greater dignity for the acting profession, urging that it have a legitimate place in society. The brief sojourn at Sabbioneta may have given Cecchini his initial inspiration. In his published works, he not only provides us with insights into the playing of the *commedia* and the nature of the various masks, but he also argues for making the theatre into a social and artistic institution. He at one time had the audacity to refuse to carry out the order of his patron, Duke Vincenzo Gonzaga of Mantua, that he merge his Accesi Company with the Fedeli: "Please believe me, your Illustrious Highness, that we run risks of breaking up the company, of raising issues for the city, of creating continual rancor, and of causing who knows what other ill. Hence it would be good advice that your Highness leave the matter of uniting or breaking companies to the players" (quoted in Carandini 1990, 122). In his *Breve discorso intorno alle commedie, commedianti e spettatori* (Brief Discourse on Plays, Players, and Spectators, 1614), he postulated an alternative system for the theatrical life of a city modeled on the economic system of Florence of the time. Indeed, he claims that Florence had already granted the art of acting an equal standing with the other arts and given it its own guild: "No one," he says, "shall then be allowed to perform if not enrolled as either master or apprentice and no government agency can prevent or impede the performance of duly enrolled players" (Cecchini [1614] 1957–61, 3:364). This passage is one of the earliest references to acting as an *"arte"* (profession), well before the form took on the label of *commedia dell'arte*. In his study of Cecchini's career, Cesare Molinari declares himself unable to discover any historical evidence for this Florentine acting guild (Molinari 1983, 6–7). At any rate, Cecchini himself clearly saw theatre as a civic institution that should be incorporated and protected by the city-state.

If indeed Cecchini had acted in the ducal company assembled by Silvio de' Gambi and then assumed its leadership to create the Accesi, or (on the evidence of d'Ancona) had actually created the company earlier in 1590 and brought it to Sabbioneta, some of the inspiration for his vision of a more stable, state-supported institution of theatre must have derived from that brief, golden moment at the court theatre of Duke Vespasiano Gonzaga. At any rate, the Teatro all'Antica stands today in the middle of the quiet, bucolic town of Sabbioneta as a quaint and fascinating reminder of a noble but brief experiment: a resident *commedia* theatre.

Works Cited

(All quotations above are translated by the author.)

Anderson, Michael. "Making Room: *Commedia* and the Privatization of the Theatre." In *The Commedia dell'Arte from the Renaissance to Dario Fo,* edited by Christopher Cairns. Lewiston: Edwin Mellen Press, 1988.

Carrandini, Silvia. *Teatro e spettacolo nel Seicento.* Bari: Editori Laterza, 1990.

Cecchini, Pier Maria. *Breve discorso intorno alle commedie. commedianti e spettatori.* 1614. Reprinted in *La Commedia dell'Arte: storia e testi,* 6 vols. Edited by Vito Pandolfi. Florence: Sansoni, 1957–61.

Craig, Edward Gordon. *Books and Theatres.* 1925. Reprint. Freeport, NY: Books for Libraries Press, 1967.

D'Ancona, Alessandro. *Le origini del teatro italiano.* 2 vols. Turin: Loescher, 1891. Reprint. Rome: Bardi Editore, 1971.

De' Dondi, Nicolò. *Estratti del Diario delle cose avvenute in Sabbioneta dal MDLXXX al MDC.* Edited by Giuseppe Muller. Milan: Francesco Colombo, 1857.

Evangelista, Anna Maria. "Il teatro dei comici d'arte a Firenze (ricognizione dello 'Stanzone delle Commedie')." *Biblioteca teatrale* 23/24 (1979): 70–86.

Mariti, Luciano. "Le collocazioni del teatro nella società barocca: dilettanti e professionisti." In *Alle origini del teatro moderno: la Commedia dell'Arte,* edited by Luciano Mariti. Rome: Bulzoni Editore, 1980.

Mazzoni, Stefano, and Ovidio Guaita. *Il teatro di Sabbioneta.* Florence: Leo S. Olschki, 1985.

Molinari, Cesare. *Un commediante e il suo mestiere*. Ferrara: Italo Bovolenta Editore, 1983.

Morinello, Cesare. "Pier Maria Cecchini." In *Enciclopedia dello spettacolo*. 9 vols. Rome: Casa Editrice le Maschere, 1955.

Sanesi, Ireneo. *La Commedia*. 2 vols. Milan: Casa Editrice Dottor Francesco Vallardi, 1935.

Solerti, Angelo. *Ferrara e la corte estense*. Città di Castello: Lapi, 1900.

Taviani, Ferdinando. *La Commedia dell'Arte e la società barocca: la fascinazione del teatro*. Rome: Mario Bulzoni Editore, 1969.

Zorzi, Ludovico. *Il teatro e la città: saggi sulla scena italiana*. Turin: Einaudi, 1977.

———. "Il Teatro Mediceo degli Uffizi e il Teatrino detto della Dogana," in *Il potere e lo spazio: la scena del principe*. Florence: Electa Editrice, 1980.

A Semiotic Interpretation of the

Lazzi of the *Commedia dell'Arte*

Anna L. Moro

HE *LAZZI* OF THE *commedia dell'arte* are generally defined as the "comic business," "comic episodes," or "comic routines" that took place on stage and that could have had, but need not have had, a relation to the plot. Mel Gordon, in his study of the *lazzi*, states that the *"lazzi* allude to any discrete, or independent, comic and repeatable activity that guaranteed laughs for its participants" (1983, 5). At times these routines arose spontaneously out of the performance—when the audience revealed signs of boredom, when the actors simply wished to add a comic routine to the scene, when *lazzi* were used as a method of masking errors; at times, their inclusion in the performance was preplanned, either to contribute to the development of the plot or to reveal the capabilities of a certain actor (Gordon 1983, 5; Lea 1934, 1:66–68; Miklaševskij 1981, 69–70). This "comic business" could have been expressed verbally or through mime, and less often through dance, song, and music (Oreglia 1968, 11). These comic episodes were certainly successful: Gordon's collection of known *lazzi* includes over two hundred routines from the mid 1500s to the mid 1700s.

What is of interest here is the relationship between the *lazzo* and the overall *commedia* performance. To attempt to identify the precise role of the *lazzo* within the *commedia dell'arte* performance is a difficult task, principally because our knowledge of the structure of individual *lazzi* is limited to brief descriptions[1] and because our appraisal of their impor-

---

[1] The only manuscript that contains a list of *lazzi* described in detail is the "Selva ovvero Zibaldone di concetti comici" by Placido Adriani of Lucca (1734), currently in the Bibli-

tance within the structure of the performance as a whole can often be based on no more than a cryptic reference in a *scenario*.[2] Opinions on the function of the *lazzi* within the framework of the performance generally fall into one or more of the following, not mutually exclusive, categories: (1) the *lazzo* serves a practical function; (2) it serves a purely comic function; (3) it serves an ornamental function; (4) the *lazzo* is an independent moment within the performance, in no way linked with the performance; (5) the *lazzo* has merely a disruptive function. Neither scholars from the time of the *commedia dell'arte* nor scholars from the twentieth century agree on a classification of the *lazzi*.

The actor and writer Pier Maria Cecchini lamented that often many of the comic characters, with their individual comic routines (*facezie*), break the continuity of the performance and cause the audience to forget the subject matter of the performance (1957–59, 4:88). Riccoboni, too, stated that the *lazzo* interrupted the scene; but he was not quite sure, since he, rather paradoxically, added that the *lazzo* was also what bound the scene together (1730, 1:68–69).[3] Among modern scholars, Nicolini maintains that the *lazzo* is to be viewed as a minor action that is inserted indecorously into a scene and that severs the main action (1958, 257). Consequently, Nicolini attributes only a practical function to the *lazzi*, such as that of alleviating audience boredom or of diverting attention away either from a novice actor who fumbled or from an actor receiving too much applause (1958, 262). Duchartre recognizes that the *lazzi* "formed a regular and important part of the entertainment," but he adds that "an actor would resort to *lazzi* whenever a scene began to drag or his eloquence gave out" and that these routines "served to keep the audience amused while the troupe took time for a breathing-spell" (1966, 36–37). Lea classifies the *lazzi* into those that delay and those that interrupt the main action (1934, 1:68–69). According to Nicoll, *lazzi* are episodes independent from the plots, "forming small oases of business which either break up the telling of the main stories or else form hilarious conclusions to each act" (1963, 144). Some critics emphasize the ornamental nature of the *lazzi*. Tessari defines the *lazzo* as a self-contained unit of performance that constitutes the spice of the play as a whole (1981,

---

oteca Comunale of Perugia (MS. A. 20). For a discussion of this manuscript, see Garfein and Gordon 1978, Thérault 1965, and Zorzi 1980.

[2]Marotti has commented specifically on this difficulty (Marotti et al. 1980, 116–17).

[3]Riccoboni's view of the "binding" function of *lazzi* is in accord with the etymology that he ascribes to the word *lazzi*: a Lombard variant of the Tuscan *lacci*, equivalent to the French *liens*. In general, it is disputed whether *lazzo* is to be attributed to *laccio* or to a variant of *l'azione;* on the etymology of *lazzo*, see Hall 1939, 41–42 and Gordon 1983, 5.

91–93). Erenstein refers to the *lazzi* as "the cherries on the *commedia dell'arte* cake" (1989, 119).

No one disputes that the immediate goal of these routines was to elicit laughter, or that they might, at times, have provided actors with a convenient way of avoiding undesirable moments on stage. But, these functions aside, were the *lazzi* merely the seasoning of the performance, episodes in no way related to the overall performance? I should like to approach the issue from a theoretical perspective to illustrate that the *lazzi* were successful because they played a more significant role within the performance than is generally attributed to them. The theoretical model I shall adopt is that proposed by Jurij Lotman in his essay on the semiotics of theatre (1981).

Lotman's central notion is the idea of opposition; according to Lotman, both the theatrical text's complexity and its significance are the result of the opposition of different elements at various levels. Our task will be to examine the *lazzi* in view of Lotman's theory of opposition and hence to determine their semiotic significance in the performance. Using some of the categories of *lazzi* outlined by Gordon in his study,[4] we shall first establish the *lazzo* as an opposition-producing unit within the performance and subsequently consider the implications of having defined it thus.

Let us begin our analysis with the concept of spatial opposition. According to Lotman, theatrical space consists of two distinct units: stage and house; these spatial units produce relationships that are the basis of certain semiotic oppositions: that of existence/nonexistence and that of significance/nonsignificance (1981, 8–9). We shall concentrate on the former relationship first and return to the latter opposition afterwards.

Lotman's existence/nonexistence opposition is based on the premise that there are two dimensions of reality at work within theatrical space. The audience relinquishes its reality but embraces the illusory reality of the stage; thus, all that exists for the audience is the stage reality. From the point of view of the actors on stage, the audience does not exist; yet, at the same time, the performance depends upon the audience's reaction (1981, 8–10). The latter notion is certainly significant in a discussion of routines that evidently developed in reaction to audience response. And although it is true that in performances of the *commedia dell'arte* space was not always well defined—critics often mention that performances

---

[4]Gordon groups over 200 known *lazzi* into twelve categories. Unless otherwise stated, the *lazzi* analyzed in this paper are found in Gordon's collection. Although Gordon's work does not constitute a critical study of *lazzi,* it is a useful compilation of them, and it is the only one available in English.

were given in *piazze,* for example, where such elements as house, stage, curtains, and lighting, the constituent parts required for the spatial opposition, could not have been present—Lotman observes that a spectator is aware of the boundary between stage reality and audience reality even if such a boundary is less defined than it is in modern theatre (1981, 8).

Lotman's theory is interesting in view of those *lazzi* that Gordon classifies as *stage/life duality.* These *lazzi* add a further dimension to the spatial opposition outlined by Lotman. As Gordon states, the *stage/life duality lazzi* "break the seams of the dramatic illusion"; they "toy with the scenic conventions of the actor-audience relationship" (1983, 41). These, in general, acknowledge audience presence. For example, in the *lazzo of the chase,* the Captain chases Coviello; as they mime running, they acknowledge audience response. In the *lazzo of the script,* Arlecchino addresses the audience directly when his jokes receive no laughter. The *lazzo of the interruption* consists of a routine in which, during a scene, offstage actors step into the audience and shout nonsensical comments at their partners on stage. In another *lazzo (lazzo of the dead),* Pulcinella rises from the dead periodically during the performance to inform the audience that it is not to disturb the dead. This type of *lazzo* undercuts the usual actor/stage-audience/house relationship and, in so doing, creates further spatial opposition within the performance.

Lazzi may also oppose the performance through thematic content. Let us consider the *lazzi* that are placed under the headings *comic violence/ sadistic behaviour* and *social-class rebellion.* Gordon indicates the thematic content of these: "subconscious . . . retribution or retaliation" and "class reversal" (1983, 14; 37). He refers to the fact that in these *lazzi* we find *commedia* themes overturned. A leitmotif of *commedia* performances, especially the earlier ones, was the abuse suffered by the *zanni* at the hands of their masters. Decroisette, in a study of the figure of the *zanni,* speaks of the "repression" and "submission" of the *zanni;* she recognizes in the figure of the *zanni* the "centre of a theatrical metaphor," which represents the traditional relationship between the oppressed and the oppressor and which makes reference to the Venetian social situation (1985, 77). Gordon speaks of the "subjugation and punishment of the innocent or defenseless" in the "world of masters and servants" (1983, 14). Thus, we many identify the theme of the social repression of the *zanni* as a refrain in the composition of *commedia* performances, and the reversal of this theme as a dominant chord in certain *lazzi.* The *comic violence/sadistic behaviour lazzi* and the *social-class rebellion lazzi* provide us with examples of the servant figure avenging himself; the *zanni* either inflicts pain or some form of retribution on his master, or simply disobeys him: the *lazzo of the shampoo,* the *lazzo of the knock,* the *lazzo of "God give you Joy,"* the *lazzo of the innocent by-stander,* the *lazzo of "Why don't you?",* the *lazzo of shut up.* These routines communicate a message that contrasts with the message conveyed by the performance. Thus, we have thematic opposition between the *lazzo* and the overall performance.

Lazzi that are classified by Gordon under the headings *illogical, food,* and *stupidity/inappropriate behaviour* produce another type of opposition within the performance: an opposition to the plot structure. We take our point of departure from Gordon's observation that the *food lazzi* represent the infant's search for nourishment and that this type of routine, in which the *zanni* often behaves in a "messy" fashion, "contrasts with other plot developments, such as the higher romantic states of the lovers or even the complicated schemes of the master characters" (1983, 21). These routines consist of such acts as Pedrolino appearing from a large pie *(lazzo of the pie),* the snatching of food from the mouths of female characters *(lazzo of snatching food from their mouths),* and Arlecchino emptying the Captain's glass of wine with a straw *(lazzo of the straw).* This type of *lazzo* opposes the plot structure not only through its infantile quality, but also by introducing trivial or everyday elements such as food or drink into the plot.

If we may consider the *food lazzi* as forming an opposition to the structure of the plot, so too may we consider the *stupidity/inappropriate behaviour lazzi* and the *illogical lazzi.* To these categories belong those *lazzi* that "violate" the rules of "human interaction" (Gordon 1983, 43). These *lazzi* seem to have no logical foundation: characters suddenly forget how to hold swords *(lazzo of cowardice),* a servant seems incapable of finding something that is in front of his eyes *(lazzo of looking everywhere and finding nothing),* the "Doctor mispronounces Pantalone's name in various insulting ways and then asks for the sexual favours of his daughter or wife" *(lazzo of the insult).* How do these nonsensical and irrational acts oppose the plot?

Let us examine briefly the structure of the plot and the structure of *commedia* performances in general. In order to do so, we must understand first the structure of the *canovaccio.* Zorzi has schematized the morphology of the typical *canovaccio* and has emphasized its "rigidity." This rigidity is the result of its fixed elements: the "fixed roles" *(parti fisse)*—four central serious roles, four peripheral comic roles—the seriousness of the dramatic situations and the symmetrical relationships between the characters.[5] The *canovaccio* represents the frame around

---

[5]Zorzi's famous schema of the typical *canovaccio* illustrates the overall symmetrical pattern of possible relationships between the principal characters of the *commedia dell'arte.* Horizontal vectors show the relationships between the four "serious" characters (the two

which the *commedia* performance was constructed and to which a performer could introduce only a limited number of variations (Zorzi 1983, 70). From these observations and from Tessari's discussion on the construction of *commedia* performances (1981, 75–95), it appears that the performance evolved within a framework of fixed possibilities. To a large extent, all the principal elements of the performance were stock: the plot, the verbal component, the characters; therefore, among so many fixed, or stock elements, the story line could not but move in a fixed number of directions. As Tessari observes, *commedia* plots were infinite variations of the same story (1981, 86). The spectator knew in essence how the plot would unravel; he did not know the details, but he knew what type of story line to expect. It is precisely for this reason that Lotman once referred to the *commedia dell'arte* as a type of art characterized by the "aesthetics of identity," that is, a type of art in which the characters are constructed around the principle of identity (since the characters are always the same) and whose artistic effect hinges on the fact that the spectator knows the nature of the characters before attending the performance (1970, 78). The spectator, by knowing the nature of the characters, knew the nature of the plot development, since the characters could be expected only to perform within the limits of their characteristics. Yet, as Lotman points out, in order for the aesthetics of identity not to lose its ability to communicate information, it must be able to infuse diversity into the unchanging elements (1970, 79). Indeed, it is not surprising that many scholars have emphasized that the technique of improvisation in the *commedia dell'arte* is to be viewed not so much as a creative process, but rather as a compositional process:[6] an ability akin to that of putting together a limited number of building blocks in a new way each time so as to produce always a fresh design.

The use of the type of routine that belongs to the *illogical lazzi* and the *stupidity/inappropriate behaviour lazzi* constitutes a method of introducing the unexpected or the unpredictable into the design of the plot structure. One might say that any *lazzo* could fulfill this function; however, this type of *lazzo* opposes the plot structure in a particular way: its illogical quality contrasts with the very determined, or logical, development of the general story line. This type of *lazzo* is not founded upon logic; therefore, its structure—or lack of structure—is directly opposed to the set structure of the plot.

---

pairs of lovers), while a series of transversal lines indicates the various asymmetrical relationships (familial, economic, social, sexual) between the individual characters (1983, 70; see also above, p. 49).

[6]See Tessari (1969, 224), Marotti et al. (1980, 120–21), and Pietropaolo (1989).

A further opposition that needs to be considered is that of character. As is evident from Gordon's study, several *lazzi* focus on certain characters of the *commedia dell'arte*. Since the characters that partake of the *lazzi* are those of the *commedia dell'arte* in general, we cannot say that the *lazzi* reveal character types that are not present in the main performance; rather, we may only say that a number of *lazzi* are used as a mechanism through which certain character types are crystallized. Insofar as this theatrical mechanism has the function of underscoring the traits of certain characters more than the general performance would permit, we may perceive it to have a function that contrasts with that of the overall performance.

Let us examine the *trickery lazzi* and the *sexual/scatological lazzi* from this perspective. The *trickery lazzi* "established a division of character type: the eternal schemers like Pulcinella and the eternal dupes like Pantalone and Arlecchino" (Gordon 1983, 51). In these routines, Pulcinella obtains what he desires by successfully outwitting other characters, such as the creditor or some guards *(lazzo of paying, lazzo of the flour, lazzo of the goodness of Pulcinella)*; Pantalone is made to look foolish by his wife as she succeeds in diverting her husband's attention so that her lover may flee *(lazzo of the tart)*; the *zanni* appear to be idiots at the mercy of thieves *(lazzo of the card game, lazzo of rubbing up against him, lazzo of the country of Cuccagna)*; Arlecchino is duped by Triviello, another *zanni (lazzo of the living corpse)*. The *sexual/scatological lazzi* evidently "were among the most popular routines" (Gordon 1983, 32). These *lazzi* involve vomiting *(lazzo of vomit)*, urinating *(lazzo of urinating on her)*, mimicry of sexual acts *(lazzo of looking to measure her)*, and various other obscenities. Gordon is careful to point out that these *lazzi* belong solely to the *zanni*. So, too, do many of the *acrobatic and mimic lazzi*, which comprise much climbing, falling, gymnastics, and mimicry of animal movements (as in the *lazzo of somersaults* and the *lazzo of the cat*). The *lazzi* that have just been described place into focus distinct features of certain characters— Pantalone, and in most cases, the *zanni*. Through these *lazzi*, these characters are set up to contrast with other characters; their traits are emphasized against the traits of the lovers, for example. The opposition that we are identifying is one of specificity/less-specificity between the *lazzo* and the performance, respectively. The *lazzo* has the function of concentrating on specific features of certain characters.

Thus far we have looked briefly at a few types of *lazzi*, attempting to identify in them an oppositional feature. We have not discussed a danger that one might face in doing this: that of considering the *lazzo* a unit outside of the performance, since it contrasts with the performance on various levels. Although the *lazzo* does present elements that oppose elements within the overall performance, it remains nevertheless a unit *within* the performance. Tim Fitzpatrick is one scholar who protests against the idea that the *lazzo* is a "deviation from the action" (1989, 186). As Lotman observes, the fact that many elements are at work independently within theatre is precisely that which gives meaning and unity to theatre (1981, 19). The *lazzo* is a unit, or a subtext, which has an independent role, but at the same time, it is integral to the performance.

We must identify the significance of the *lazzi* oppositions within performances of the *commedia dell'arte*. We have already considered one of the oppositions that Lotman considers essential within theatre: existence/nonexistence. A second fundamental opposition is that of significance/nonsignificance. According to Lotman, theatrical space is rich with signs because the components that form the world of theatre acquire meanings well beyond their immediate significance (1981, 9). At first glance, the *lazzi* appear merely to be comic routines that serve the purpose of eliciting laughter from the audience, but this function is not the limit of their significance. The significance of the *lazzi* stems from the fact that elements within them contrast with various elements of the performance. For example, the thematic opposition to which we referred serves to underscore a social situation. The routines in which the servant is no longer the victim of his master, but the one rendering his master the victim, communicate a social message. Perhaps these routines communicate a need for change in society. The *lazzi* that place emphasis on character types call attention to societal class distinctions. The *sexual/scatological lazzi* are also significant from a social viewpoint; these may be regarded in the same light in which Molinari views the erotic scenes between Zanni and the maidservant: as a type of "*pendant* caricaturale-grottesco" of the scenes that depict sublime love, as a counterpart to the celestial love of the serious characters (1985, 26). The *sexual/scatological lazzi* portray the burlesque side of the love of the more noble characters; the eroticism and obscenities of these comic episodes ridicule the story of the lovers; and, since the lovers represent a higher level of society, these routines, performed mainly by the *zanni*, poke fun at the higher class in that they undermine the virtuousness of their sublimer love. Peterson-Royce has commented on a type of *lazzo* contained within the *scenari* of the Museo Correr, in which "Zanni and Argentina . . . echo the love scenes between the high characters" (1986, 82). But if the "echoing" is done in a *lazzo*, then the perspective is comic, the effect is that of parody, and the love story of the "high characters" is reduced to a comic level. Can we not interpret this type of *lazzo* from a social point of view as well? Finally, let us consider those *lazzi* that we identified as contrasting with the plot structure. To infuse a nonsensical, unpredictable comic routine in the middle of a serious, predictable plot line constitutes not only a means of introducing the unexpected into that which is otherwise anticipated, but also a method of undermining the very seriousness of that plot line.

If we agree that the *lazzi* may communicate various levels of meaning—from basic comic significance to various degrees of social significance—then we must agree that this communication is possible through opposition. And, in attributing significance to the *lazzi,* we attribute a signlike quality to them. We have arrived at what Lotman defines as an "abundance of meaning." An "abundance of meaning" is possible in the theatrical world because of the signlike quality of its components and because of the different perspectives—the actor's, the spectator's—that interpret elements that have various degrees of signlike quality. In the world of theatre, objects stand for themselves and objects become signs for something else. From a structural point of view, elements appear syntagmatically—in a certain order—and paradigmatically, through the levels of meaning they convey. This fundamental diametric structure is what renders theatre semiotically significant; it is what gives theatre its abundance of meaning (Lotman 1981, 10–13). Thus, syntagmatically, the *lazzo* is no more than a comic routine that is inserted, spontaneously or not, within a scene. But, paradigmatically, the *lazzo* may confer other levels of meaning on the performance.

I have not made a distinction between *lazzi* that were improvised and *lazzi* that were preplanned. It is very difficult, if not impossible, to determine from a *scenario* whether or not a *lazzo* was improvised. We know that the *lazzi* were fixed comic routines; the matter of spontaneity or improvisation concerned only their insertion in the performance. We infer from Andrea Perrucci's discussion of the duties of the director of a company that indeed some of the *lazzi* were planned beforehand (1961, 263–64). Whether or not a *lazzo* was improvised is inconsequential; what matters is that the routine seemed to be improvised, that it appeared to be a break from the plot structure. By seeming to be a unit independent of the general performance, a routine could present more successfully oppositional elements with respect to the performance and could thus function effectively as a message-producing component of the performance.

Lotman has remarked that merely to describe the substructure of a text is an incomplete exercise, for it does not permit one to perceive the "dynamic" quality of a text, the "energy" of a text; in order to perceive these qualities it is essential to identify the relationships at work within the text (1974). In identifying the *lazzo* as an opposition-producing component of the *commedia dell'arte* performance, I have attempted to elucidate some of the relationships at work between this component and the text. The opposition-producing quality of the *lazzo* at various levels of the performance—at the levels of space, theme, plot, character—serves to render the performance semiotically significant. The *lazzo* is a message-producing sign within the framework of the performance. Through its oppositional nature, the *lazzo* is also a component within the performance that gives the performance its dynamic quality, its energy. It is perhaps for these reasons that the duration of these comic routines paralleled the duration of the tradition of the *commedia dell'arte*.

Works Cited

Cecchini, Pier Maria. "Discorso sopra l'arte comica con il modo di ben recitare." In *La commedia dell'arte: Storia e testi*, edited by Vito Pandolfi. 6 vols. Florence: Sansoni, 1957–59.

Decroisette, Françoise. "Le zanni ou la métaphore de l'opprimé dans la Commedia dell'Arte." *Figures théâtrales du peuple*, 75–90. Paris: Centre National de la Recherche Scientifique, 1985.

Duchartre, Pierre Louis. *The Italian Comedy*. Translated by Randolph T. Weaver. 1929. Reprint. New York: Dover Publications, 1966.

Erenstein, Robert L. "The Humour of the *Commedia dell'Arte*." In *The* Commedia dell'Arte *from the Renaissance to Dario Fo*, edited by Christopher Cairns, 118–40. Lewiston: Mellen, 1989.

Fitzpatrick, Tim. "Flaminio Scala's Prototypal Scenarios: Segmenting the Text/Performance." In *The Science of Buffoonery: Theory and History of the* Commedia dell'Arte, edited by Domenico Pietropaolo, 177–98. Ottawa: Dovehouse, 1989.

Garfein, Herschel, and Mel Gordon. "The Adriani *Lazzi* of the *Commedia dell'Arte*." *The Drama Review* 22:1 (1978): 3–12.

Gordon, Mel. Lazzi: *The Comic Routines of the* Commedia dell'Arte. New York: Performing Arts Journal, 1983.

Hall, Robert A. "Italian Etymological Notes." *Language* 15 (1939): 34–42.

Lea, Kathleen M. *Italian Popular Comedy*. 2 vols. Oxford: Clarendon, 1934.

Lotman, Jurij M. "Le Hors-Texte." In *La poétique la mémoire*, translated by Leon Robel, 68–81. Paris: Seuil, 1970.

———. "On Some Principal Difficulties in the Structural Description of Text." *Linguistics* 121 (1974): 57–63.

———. "Semiotica della scena." Translated by Simonetta Salvestroni. *Strumenti Critici* 15:1 (1981): 1–29.

Marotti, Ferruccio et al. "Interventi." In *La Commedia dell'arte: Atti del convegno di studi. Pontedera 28–30 maggio 1976*, edited by Luciano Mariti, 116–25. Rome: Bulzoni, 1980.

Miklaševskij, Konstantin. *La Commedia dell'Arte o il teatro dei commedianti italiani nei secoli XVI, XVII e XVIII*. Translated by Carla Solivetti. 1914–17. Venice: Marsilio, 1981.

Molinari, Cesare. *La commedia dell'arte*. Milan: Mondadori, 1985.

Nicolini, Fausto. *Vita di Arlecchino*. Milan: Ricciardi, 1958.

Nicoll, Allardyce. *The World of Harlequin*. Cambridge: Cambridge University Press, 1963.

Oreglia, Giacomo. *The* Commedia dell'Arte. Translated by Lovett F. Edwards. Rev. ed. 1964. Reprint. New York: Methuen, 1968.

Perrucci, Andrea. *Dell'arte rappresentativa premeditata ed all'improvviso*. Edited by Anton Giulio Bragaglia. Florence: Sansoni, 1961.

Peterson-Royce, Anya. "The Venetian *Commedia:* Actors and Masques in the Development of the *Commedia dell'Arte.*" *Theatre Survey* 27:1/2 (1986): 69–87.

Pietropaolo, Domenico. "Improvisation as a Stochastic Composition Process." In *The Science of Buffoonery: Theory and History of the* Commedia dell'Arte, edited by Domenico Pietropaolo, 167–75. Ottawa: Dovehouse, 1989.

Riccoboni, Luigi. *Histoire du théâtre italien*. 2 vols. Paris, 1730.

Tessari, Roberto. *Commedia dell'Arte: la maschera e l'ombra*. Milan: Mursia, 1981.

———. *La commedia dell'arte nel Seicento: "Industria" e "arte giocosa" nella civiltà barocca*. Florence: Olschki, 1969.

Thérault, Suzanne. *La Commedia dell'arte vue à travers le Zibaldone de Pérouse*. Paris: Centre National de la Recherche Scientifique, 1965.

Zorzi, Ludovico. "La raccolta degli scenari italiani della Commedia dell'Arte." In *La Commedia dell'arte: Atti del convegno di studi. Pontedera 28–30 maggio 1976*, edited by Luciano Mariti, 105–15. Rome: Bulzoni, 1980.

———. "Intorno alla Commedia dell'Arte." In *Arte della maschera nella Commedia dell'Arte*, edited by Donato Sartori and Bruno Lanata, 63–83. Florence: Usher, 1983.

Watteau's *Commedia* and the Theatricality of French Painting

Michael L. Quinn

*T*HE THEATRICALITY of Jean-Antoine Watteau's paintings remains one of the intractable problems of French art history. The works' most intriguing character images are clearly from the theatre, and their mode of presentation conforms to many of the characteristics of painting that have since been described as "theatrical," yet the sources of his scenes and the contexts of their use remain as indistinct as the very idea of "theatricality" that is used to distance the paintings from reality. Rather than view the theatricality of Watteau's work as a source of iconographic solutions to the paintings' mysteries, or as a problem that must be overcome by interpretation, I would like to offer the paradox of theatricality in painting as a central theme in Watteau's work and argue for its historical importance in the emerging discourse on theatrical painting in eighteenth-century France.

In the course of a twenty-year career, during a time when the *commedia dell'arte* had been exiled from Paris, Watteau managed to establish a revolution in genre painting that was the culmination of the French rococo style and that redefined the relation of painting to theatre. Michael Fried has argued convincingly that a controversy over the theatrical implications of painting, as initiated in the salons of Diderot and the theories of Rousseau, provided the dominant formal dialectic in French art from Greuze through David (1980, 1–2). Of the French artists doing theatrical paintings, Watteau offers a crucial artistic precedent for the philosophical arguments about theatrical painting that began at mid-century; his busy life and early death predate Diderot's first salon by more than two decades, and during the interim his work was collected with great energy and appreciated in value enormously. By focusing on the theatrical gestures implicit in Watteau's technique, the problematic theatrical sources and social relations of his paintings, and the difficulty of their interpretation, I suggest that Watteau's mature paintings, and especially those involving characters related to the *commedia dell'arte,* constitute an early crisis point in the theatricality of painting. Though often praised for their simplicity, Watteau's illusive canvases offer such an intensely reflexive theatricality that they express irresolvable contradictions, conforming to the pattern of paradoxical representational deferral that deconstructive critics describe as a *mise-en-abyme.*

Comédie de l'atelier

Watteau was born in the north, the home of genre painting, in the town of Valenciennes, the most famous theatre-historical site of the medieval *décor-simultanée.* Watteau's early contact with genre painting, the matter of everyday life in art, put him in a position to challenge the primacy of history painting in the French tradition; from a theatrical standpoint, the images of genre painting have access to an empirical argument for representational truth that was never part of the idealized narrative contexts for truth that underlie representation in the history painting tradition. Oliver Banks has demonstrated that Watteau's mature themes can be traced in precedents from the Dutch genre traditions, yet the crucial factor in Watteau's reception and in the theatrical paintings seems to be that his position as a genre painter in a history painting tradition constructs for his work the possibility of a dialogue between two kinds of truth claims (1977). This dialogic structure corresponds to such theatrical problems as the paradox of acting, later celebrated by Diderot, in which the spectator never knows the extent to which the actor shares the sentiments of the character being performed (1957).

The stage practice of simultaneous settings used a system of "mansions" and open areas that allowed a freedom of narrative movement in medieval religious drama (Kernodle 1944). If a passion like the one historically performed at Valenciennes required several settings, they were all constructed as relatively distinct parts of a large set, in which all the scenes of the story were shown at once while the actors moved among them. The scene, in medieval art, corresponds to what Erich Auerbach calls a "figura," an image rooted in a narrative but capable of a constructive reference forward and backward in time through many different scenes and historical contexts (1973). This practice of simultaneous decor continued in the French theatre through the seventeenth century, so that the notion of a discrete, organic, background setting, carefully matched to a single scene in the play being performed, was not the ordinary assumption of theatrical design that it is today.[1] Watteau's use of *commedia* characters in different scenic contexts responds to a different theatrical aesthetic than many modern critics, arguing from contemporary theatre practice, have supposed.[2]

At eighteen Watteau went to Paris, apparently in the company of a scene painter, and about two years later, in 1704, he entered the studio of Claude Gillot. As one of the community of Flemish painters in Paris, Watteau was set to work painting merchandise for the fair booths, churning out images in a busy studio that was more like a production line than an academy. The primary product was the patron saint, or some other figural icon; some apprentices specialized in parts of the body, or technical problems like drapery, but Watteau painted whole figures like Saint Nicholas, which he apparently knew by heart and could render without a model (Crow 1985, 45). At the very beginning of his career, then, Watteau mastered a large repertory of figures and poses and could reproduce them with remarkable speed. In one surviving painting that the two artists apparently executed together—implying that Gillot was in charge—the product, *Harlequin, Emperor of the Moon,* seems very close to theatre illustration, for Harlequin, a standard figure from *commedia dell'arte,* is apparently recorded as he appeared in Nolant de Fatouville's play, performed at the St. Laurent fair in 1707 (Goodden 1986, 84). Watteau's talent for figure-drawing was also exercised in numerous costume plates, and a "suite of figures invented by Watteau" that was eventually engraved by Caylus (Michel 1984, 256–57).

Gillot was probably the French painter most passionately interested in the *commedia dell'arte* since Callot—so interested that his work was often not so much a commentary upon the stage as it was a kind of "theatrical illustration," designed to capture the moment on stage in a drawing or painting that recorded costumes and scenery in arresting detail. As theatre-historical documents, Gillot's images are probably much more useful than Watteau's, though few of the older artist's works survive. But even in the Watteau painting most clearly indebted to Gillot, *The Departure of the Italian Comedians in 1697,* this documentary approach to theatrical painting is wholly lacking (fig. 1). The actors in the painting

---

[1]See examples of these settings in Mahelot 1920.

[2]Perhaps the most extreme example is Hollander 1989, which takes as its premise the possibilities of the modern motion picture for the analysis of implied narrative and movement in painting. However, Hollander's choice is not naive, and her analysis of costume in Watteau is extremely interesting.

Figure 1. The Departure of the Italian Comedians in 1697, engraving after Watteau (51.3 x 62.1 cm.), London, Trustees of the British Museum.

left Paris five years before the artist arrived; consequently, the image seems to be composed of figures taken from Gillot, rendered in the poses he used to characterize the actors' performances, then strangely transported to the scene of their exile. The resulting image, which survives only in an engraving, is as likely to be a parody of Gillot's nostalgia for the Italians, in the grotesque style of the satires from the fair theatres, as it is to be the historical "theatre painting" that so many modern historians reproduce without comment in studies of the *commedia dell'arte.*[3] The compositional strategy of quoting prearranged figures and recombining them in different settings has firm precedents in French painting in the legacy of LeBrun and his work on the passions, but the compositional gesture Watteau uses to create his "tribute to Gillot" also imitates with delirious cognitive results the active, recombinant, creative princi-

---

[3]See for example Richards and Richards 1990, 8.

ples of the *commedia dell'arte,* and of their Parisian rump, the theatres of the fair.

Watteau soon left Gillot's workhouse for another, that of Audran, who specialized in arabesque ornaments for interior design. In this decorative studio Watteau began to construct figures in compositional dialogue and learned a style of composition utterly at odds with modern conceptions of visionary, organic painting. Designs were done to order; some sections were left blank, so as to be filled in with images of the client's choice. The finished product was not a solitary image for concentrated display or sentimental identification, but a stylistic surround—a whole room in which the painting was both everywhere and nowhere in particular. The use of facing mirrors was one of the favorite techniques of the rococo interior, constructing the deferral of painted surfaces into the *mise-en-abyme* in which the room, its ornaments, and the beholder between the mirrors are infinitely extended in the repeating mirror images. These compositional gestures of the social surround, the interior setting for ordinary bourgeois life, seem to have been reconstituted as outdoor themes for Watteau. When he was able to leave Audran for an independent career, the deconstructive challenges of the ornament (Derrida's *parergon*) and the theatrical *mise-en-abyme* emerge as fully realized aspects of the later works (Derrida 1987).

Full Frontal Theatricality

Watteau's blend of Flemish genre painting and theatrical illustration seems to have formed in a set of works involving *commedia* images between 1709, when he left Audran to make his first unsuccessful bid to the Academy, and 1712, when the Academicians offered him the rare privilege of choosing his own accession subject. The breakthrough painting seems to have been *The Jealous Ones,* soon after reworked into *Pierrot Content* (fig. 2). Most critics, like Donald Posner, have been struck by the extent to which Watteau remains free from the authority of the theatre in these paintings, inventing a scene that has few specific narrative suggestions but that captures something vital in its impression of theatricality (1984, 56). When looking at the two versions, one now lost except in engraving, art historians have tended to focus on their differences. Yet it seems to me that the most striking aspect of both paintings is the central figure, Pierrot, an image from the theatre of the fair.[4] Pierrot provides a strong, fascinating central point of focus that throws the others into

---

[4]The actor who played Pierrot, Hamoche, worked at Saint Laurent despite efforts to move to a more legitimate venue. See Welsford 1961, 308.

Figure 2. Pierrot Content (35 x 31 cm.), Lugano, Thyssen-Bornemisza Collection.

balanced dialogue, yet he nevertheless focuses full front, looking at the beholder rather than at the others in the painting. This confrontation of Pierrot with the audience, which leaps out from these early paintings, is repeated in a few other images that test it through simplicity of presentation and through its use in much more complex images.

When Michael Fried talks about theatricality in painting, he tends to distinguish between figures that are absorbed in their own behavior, like those in his favorite canvasses by Chardin, and those that look out from the painting in gestures of self-conscious display.[5] Pierrot, or Gilles as he is sometimes called, does both things at once; he looks out from the canvas, but he is absorbed in the looking—he is not anxious about his ontology but is content to look forward with the perspective of a theatricality that is removed from any institutional theatrical context. His illusive look is the graphic sign of the emergent crisis of theatricality in French painting, like that which Manet's *Olympia* would later use as a retort to her own nakedness (Clark 1985), and which Jean-Paul Sartre would eventually theorize for our own era, in *Being and Nothingness,* as the phenomenology of the gaze (1966). Watteau, Caylus tell us, painted the whole background first, and then the characters over the top, and radiography shows that Watteau often made substantial adjustments of his background scenes without changing the placement of the figures on the painting (Posner 1984, 162–64). By building up from a dark sizing coat to the final layers of white, Watteau caused the figure of Pierrot to seem to float on the surface of the canvas like an actor on the front edge of a drop, only a transparent shimmer of varnish between his supposedly artificial world and the more sizable, less congenial life of the viewer. In a later painting, *The Foursome,* in which Pierrot turns his back, it is the loss of this gaze that still dominates the painting, while in a painting in which Pierrot is less crucial, like *The Pleasures of the Ball,* the glance from his small figure still comes forward from the back of a marginal group—at the edge of the drop?—with remarkable power. Some iconographers have struggled to interpret this gazing figure as the sign of some other narrative character, perhaps an *Ecce Homo* in the figure of the holy fool; such a displacement of the clear, discrete, conventional sign of the *commedia* figure seems to me to be based in the depth of this theatrical effect, which the gazing Christ also often uses.[6] Long-standing attempts to explain the absence of movement in these figures through the imagina-

---

[5]Chardin is compared favorably to almost everyone, and especially to Greuze and Boucher, in Fried's first chapter, "The Primacy of Absorption" (1980, 7–70).

[6]This reading was suggested during the symposium; see Storey 1978 for a survey of iconographical materials on the Pierrot figure.

tion of a verbal theatre of *marivaudage*, like Mary Paula Vidal's current attempts to explain theatricality by collapsing it into "conversation," are unable to account for the singularity of Pierrot's gaze, which may allow a responding look, but does not necessarily require one, and certainly does not imply speech (Tomlinson 1981; Vidal 1988).

Coups de théâtre

Thomas Crow argues persuasively that Watteau's *fêtes galantes* (a term coined to describe his work when Watteau entered the Academy) capture an ongoing dialogue that existed in French culture between the supposedly low art of the fair theatres, particularly of the short parades that were designed to persuade customers outside the theatre to buy a ticket, and the erotic, costumed masquerades of the wealthy upper class (1985, 54). But Watteau, in close sympathy with neither social group, intrudes a regular series of *coups de théâtre* into the festive scenes of social masquer-

Figure 3. The Delights of Life (69 x 90 cm.), London, Trustees of the Wallace Collection.

Figure 4. Country Amusements (128 x 193 cm.), London, Trustees of the Wallace Collection.

ade. Norman Bryson has noticed, for example, that in *The Concert* the bucolic group of figures is backed by a kind of roll-trimmed drop; in *The Delights of Life,* the same basic figures are then framed by a proscenium arch (1981, 80; fig. 3). In a series of related Arcadian romances, a voluptuous sculpture, dead when she appeared in Poussin's *Et in arcadia ego,* seems to wake from her slumber on the tomb with considerable sensuous charm, like so many theatrical statues in the tradition of transformation that stretches from Shakespeare through Molière to Gozzi and the rest (fig. 4, *Country Amusements*). When Watteau begins with a simple motif, it tends to have within it a theatrical potential and to gather meaning in development through the layering of theatrical ambiguities. Bryson, strangely, argues that the paintings create a "semantic vacuum" (1981, 65); I would suggest instead that this pronounced intertextuality of images—from theatre, classical sources, popular icons, and the system of the artist's own works—offers such an abundance of interpretive opportunities that it is hard for the imagination, caught in the dialogue of look and glance, ever to come to rest in one interpretive perspective—one determinate reading of theatrical paradox.

Another consistent element in Fried's dialectic of absorption and theatricality is the way absorbed paintings tend to play with compositional
depth, to displace the glance within their own picture planes, while
theatrical paintings tend to spread across the canvas on one level, as the
actors turn out in proscenium positions for easy viewing.[7] Paradoxically,
Chardin's absorbed depth is painted with a very thin layer of paint, while
the theatricality of an artist like Boucher requires great, deep textures of
intense color, heavy on a larger surface. Watteau shows a remarkable
ability to use the idea of theatricality to create depth, to invent illusions
of vanishing perspective or of extensive conversational depth even when
the characters sometimes seem to be painted on a backdrop, or a *mise-en-
abyme* of retreating backdrops, as in his *Country Amusements* (fig. 4).
And as Bryson notes, in paintings like *The Delights of Life* (fig. 3), Watteau is able to manipulate the details of the brushwork to a remarkable
extent within the same plane, creating a strange tension between the
glossy precision of the cello's image and the brushy energy of the little
girl next to it (1981, 80).

Watteau seems to resolve the dialectical antinomies of theatricality
because he precedes them; they only emerge as antitheses in the context
of the critic's struggle to resolve the challenge of his work to interpretation. The spatiality of the rococo style that Watteau mastered was not
an active movement toward historical completion, as in the baroque's
familiar narratives, but a "still movement," in Murray Krieger's ekphrastic
terms, toward a dissolution so intensive that it does not transcend
through noumenal otherworldliness, but through imaginative complexity (Krieger 1967, 105–28). The recent controversy over the interpretation of Watteau's Academy subject, *Pilgrimage to Cythera* (fig. 5),
demonstrates this intensive ambiguity. Though there were four versions
of this story enacted in contemporary theatres, there is no evidence that
any one of them influenced Watteau. Traditionally the painting has been
interpreted in relation to its lyric subject, and the characters are viewed as
beginning a journey to the land of love; trying to explain the melancholy
mood of the painting, Michael Levey suggests more recently that the
characters have just completed their pilgrimage to Cythera, and are on
their way home (1961, 180–85). And typically, Watteau did not paint
one *Cythera*, but two, vastly different in color and background scene, and
with different titles; the second is called *Embarkation for Cythera*. So
maybe both readings are right (though which for which painting still

---

[7]Fried's analysis of the blindness theme in David's *Belisarius* is exemplary in this respect
(1980, 155–56).

Figure 5. Pilgrimage to Cythera (129 x 193 cm.), Paris, Louvre.

remains a mystery), and there is no *stable* outside context through which the intensive internal complexities of the paintings can be resolved.

The Sign of Reflection

If there is an analytic insight to be gained from Watteau, then, it must be in this ongoing play with interpretive duplicity, in which he often portrays the paradox of the *comédien*. When he gives us a theatrical painting that seems to illustrate a single scene, like his *Comédiens français*, even the simple matter of genre, so basic to French neoclassic performance, remains ambiguous. The painting seems to show a scene from a single serious play, until the interpreter notices a comic Crispin lurking in the lower right, spoiling the singular presentation of a crumpled letter's "tragic" revelations with an outward-looking, skeptical gaze. When one of Watteau's paintings of the theatre seems to spread indifferently across a scene, it turns out to have a companion piece that throws each into relief, as in his *Love in the French Theatre* and *Love in the Italian Theatre*. Here the effect of ambiguity is spread out over more than one canvas, but so long as the context of the work matters to interpretation, such complementary contradictions confound definitive readings of "single" works by engaging them in a continuing reflective dialogue of differences.

Watteau's most straightforward portrait of an acting figure, *Mezzetin* (fig. 6), remains ambiguous because the actor cannot be positively identified; uncertainty about whether this figure was a professional actor or an amateur in theatrical dress overpowers any argument for historical accuracy the painting might otherwise claim. Watteau aggravates the situation by locating the receiver of Mezzetin's serenading glance outside the canvas, out of reach, and then dissolves the unity of the project by painting not one such image but three (and more), with the gaze moving off in different directions each time, in ways that are not always balanced by the implied gaze of the sensuous statue's figure. When Luigi Riccoboni brought the *commedia dell'arte* back to Paris in 1716 there was no Mezzetin among the masks; like Pierrot, the figure comes from the fair theatres, and in another painting Watteau puts Mezzetin in the frontal attitude of Pierrot, absorbing the theatricality of Mezzetin's aspect in a reference to the other, earlier painting's effect (see Beagle 1985, 33). The manner of the *foirains* seems to stay with Watteau not only in his wit, but also in his power of abstraction. One of Lesage's plays for the *Opéra comique,* for example, was a *querelle des théâtres,* in which one actor plays the *Comédie française,* another the *Opéra,* and a third the *Théâtre de la foire;* Dottore concludes that all three suffer from a too-constant diet and might diversify their styles (Runte 1986, 45–46). In Watteau, too, one figure might signify a whole company of men or a whole idea of social manners, but there is always plenty in the picture to feed the imagination.

Watteau's masterpiece of commentary on the theatricality of painting came in a self-consciously semiotic project that he completed in eight days, only a year before he finally succumbed to tuberculosis. For Gersaint, his friend, dealer, and eventual biographer, he volunteered to make a shop sign (fig. 7). The two-panel composition appears at first to be an ordinary record of a moment in a busy gallery, until the theatrical details begin piling up, and we learn that Gersaint's actual shop was perhaps a third of this room's size (Banks 1977, 231–52). The composition has incredible complexities of framing. The large painting on the right, an oval, is being shown in a remarkably theatrical way, and the viewers peer in for a closer look, not looking back at the spectator but imitating the

Figure 6. Mezzetin (55.3 x 43.2 cm.), New York, Metropolitan Museum of Art.

Figure 7. Gersaint's Shop Sign (163 x 308 cm.), Berlin, Charlottenburg Palace.

way the painting invites us to peer in at its wealth of detailed images. The group on the right reverses that gaze, giving the spectators of Watteau's work a chance to imagine what their staring faces might look like as they are absorbed by his painting. The left panel seems less complicated; the boy has brought some straw to help pack the crates. But wait, the stones under the packing look strangely like a stage, and he seems to have leaned back against the proscenium arch. The painting going into the crate is a portrait of Louis XIV, only a short while dead, but now stretched out under the clock. The surround is not a painted scene, but a scene of

paintings, reversing the entire dynamic of the theatricality of painting to ask the spectator to consider the imagery of theatre. And the two panels meet in a door that might also be a window and could even be a painting; this hall of mirrors—and there is a large one on each side—is both the heterotopia that Foucault theorized in his reading of *Las Meninas* and a four-sided *mise-en-abyme*, infinite not only in depth but also in breadth.[8]

---

[8]Foucault 1970, 3–16, and, for a reading of absolute reflection that tests the limits of Derrida's critique of representation, Gasche 1986.

This painting forms a reply, too, to *The Departure of the Italian Comedians,* which effectively began Watteau's theatrical career. The theatre is back in town, and Louis XIV, who drove it away, has finally been sent packing himself. Only the dog on the stage remains oblivious.

Works Cited

Auerbach, Erich. "Figura." Translated by Ralph Mannheim. In *Scenes from the Drama of European Literature.* Gloucester, MA: Peter Smith, 1973.

Banks, Oliver. *Watteau and the North: Studies in the Dutch and Flemish Baroque Influence on French Rococo Painting.* New York: Garland, 1977.

Beagle, Nancy Sue. "The *Théâtres de la Foire* in Early Eighteenth Century France: Analysis of *La Ceinture de Venus* by Lesage." Ph.D. diss., Stanford University, 1985.

Bryson, Norman. *Word and Image: French Painting of the* Ancien Régime. Cambridge: Cambridge University Press, 1981.

Clark, T. J. *The Painting of Modern Life: Paris in the Art of Manet and His Followers.* New York: Knopf, 1985.

Crow, Thomas. *Painters and Public Life in Eighteenth Century Paris.* New Haven, CT: Yale University Press, 1985.

Derrida, Jacques. *The Truth in Painting.* Translated by G. Bennington and I. McLeod. Chicago: University of Chicago Press, 1987.

Diderot, Denis. *The Paradox of Acting.* Translated by W. Pollock. New York: Hill & Wang, 1957.

Foucault, Michel. *The Order of Things: An Archeology of the Human Sciences.* New York: Vintage, 1970.

Fried, Michael. *Absorption and Theatricality: Painting and Beholder in the Age of Diderot.* Berkeley: University of California Press, 1980.

Gasche, Rodolphe. *The Tain of the Mirror: Derrida and the Philosophy of Reflection.* Cambridge, MA: Harvard University Press, 1986.

Goodden, Angelica. *Action and Persuasion: Dramatic Performance in Eighteenth Century France.* Oxford: Clarendon Press, 1986.

Hollander, Anne. *Moving Pictures.* New York: Knopf, 1989.

Kernodle, George. *From Art to Theater: Form and Convention in the Renaissance.* Chicago: University of Chicago Press, 1944.

Krieger, Murray. "The Ekphrastic Principle and the Still Movement of Poetry; or Lakoön Revisited." In *The Play and Place of Criticism,* 105–28. Baltimore: Johns Hopkins University Press, 1967.

Levey, Michael. "The Real Theme of Watteau's 'Embarkation for Cythera'." *Burlington Magazine* 103 (1961): 180–85.

Mahelot, Laurent. *Le Mémoire de Mahelot, Laurent et d'autres Decorateurs de l'Hôtel de Bourgogne et de la Comédie Française au XVIIe siècle.* Edited by H. C. Lancaster. Paris, 1920.

Michel, Marianne Roland. *Watteau: An Artist of the Eighteenth Century.* London: Trefoil, 1984.

Posner, Donald. *Antoine Watteau*. Ithaca, NY: Cornell University Press, 1984.

Richards, Kenneth, and Laura Richards. *The* Commedia dell'Arte: A Documentary History. New York: Basil Blackwell, 1990.

Runte, Roseann. "A Tapestry of Sensual Metaphors: The Vocabulary of Lesage's Theatre." In *Eighteenth Century French Theatre, Aspects and Contexts: Studies Presented to E. J. H. Greene,* edited by Magdy G. Badir and David J. Langdon, 44–51. Departments of Romance Languages and Comparative Literature, University of Alberta, 1986.

Sartre, Jean-Paul. *Being and Nothingness: An Essay on Phenomenological Ontology.* Translated by Hazel Barnes. New York: Washington Square Press, 1966.

Storey, Robert. *Pierrot: A Critical History of a Mask*. Princeton, NJ: Princeton University Press, 1978.

Tomlinson, Robert. *La Fête Galante: Watteau et Marivaux*. Paris and Geneva: E. Droz, 1981.

Vidal, Mary Paula. "Watteau's Painted Conversations: Art, Literature and Talk in Seventeenth and Eighteenth Century France." Ph.D. diss., University of California, Berkeley, 1988.

Welsford, Enid. *The Fool: His Social and Literary History*. Garden City, NY: Anchor, 1961.

Ebullience and Edification from a

Modern *Commediante*

Thomas A. Pallen

ORN IN UDINE in 1907, Nico Pepe later completed his *liceo* education and went to work in a bank. This article would not exist had he not left the teller's cage for the actor's stage in 1930, five years after joining the bank. For the next twenty-nine years he performed with a variety of professional theatre companies, advancing from *ultimo generico* to *primo brilliante* during the first two years of his new career. Along the way, he worked with the *Piccolo Teatro di Milano,* founded the *Teatro Stabile di Torino* and the *Teatro Stabile di Palermo,* and managed the *Teatro Atanea di Roma.* In 1959, his acting career turned a corner as he accepted an invitation to return to the *Piccolo Teatro di Milano* and join Giorgio Strehler's already long-running and far-touring production of Goldoni's *Arlecchino servitore di due padrone* in the mask of Pantalone, a role that occupied most of the following nineteen years of his life.

A scholar as well as an actor, Nico Pepe could not satisfy himself simply with playing Pantalone. He also wanted to know the history of both the *commedia dell'arte* and his own mask in particular. As a result of his studies, he wrote *Pantalone: The History of a Mask and of an Actor* in 1981. The present article contains both quotations from and paraphrases of my yet-to-be published translation of this book. Wanting his work to stand on its own in this, its first appearance in English, I have avoided comparisons to other studies of *commedia* except where Pepe has already made them in his text or notes. I have also chosen to follow Pepe's usage in referring to *commedia*'s denizens as "masks" *(maschere)* rather than characters *(personaggi).*[1]

---

[1]Pepe divided his book into two parts: the first, *La* Commedia dell'arte, *le Maschere,*

In his first chapter, "The Birth of the Actor" (*Nascita dell'attore*, 1981, 3), Pepe undertakes an analysis of the importance of *commedia dell'arte* in the overall scheme of things theatrical; Pepe first notes Vito Pandolfi's theory that improvisation was the hallmark and basis of this Italian performance genre (1981, 4).[2] He then advances his own estimation, as an actor, of *commedia*'s significance: "Its having given life to the figure of the actor as we know it today and having shown Europe how professional theatrical life should be organized" (1981, 5).[3] After briefly introducing a theme that will reappear later, the importance of language and particularly dialect in *commedia* characterization, Pepe begins his explication of the origin and development of *commedia*.

Citing Anton Giulio Bragaglia and Silvio D'Amico,[4] Pepe reaches back to Etruscan, Atellan, and early Roman theatre to seek, briefly and unsuccessfully, the roots of his subject. Skillfully somersaulting forward to the sixteenth century, Pepe explains the more precise and timely origins of *commedia*:

> In the sixteenth century, one knows, interest in art was an exclusive phenomenon of the upper social classes. The princes dominated their inferiors through the completely spectacular value of their life, including in this "spectacularity" the arts, literature and, naturally, theatre. In the palace, on certain occasions—an engagement, a wedding, a baptism, a visit from an illustrious personage—they performed ancient theatre texts in their original language for an audience of invited nobles. The male relatives of the head of the house acted and the female parts were taken by boys, noble youths, the women being enjoined by the church from presenting themselves on the stage to act plays. (1981, 10)

Had upper-class dilettantes taken all the roles in these amateur theatricals, professionalism might have waited considerably longer for its entrance cue. As Pepe notes, this was not the case: "In these . . . texts, . . . the most theatrically significant characters were often the humble ones of the servant, the porter, the parasite, the panderer. Now the noble actors, interested only in playing the highly cultured characters, refused

---

treating historical matters and the second, *Il mio* Pantalone, devoted to personal experience. This paper deals only with the first part.

[2]Pepe cited Pandolfi 1969. He notes Perrucci's birth and death dates, 1651–1704, and also identifies Perrucci as a "playwright, librettist, and *commedia dell'arte* theorist," but never gives the original publication date of this treatise.

[3]The expression *dare vita* [*a un'istituzione*], more usually translated as "to found [an institution]" seems to make more sense in a strictly literal translation here.

[4]Pepe identifies Bragaglia (1890–1960), a member of the Futurist movement, as "a total man of the theatre" in the process of quoting his "Preface" to Perrucci 1961, and also quotes from D'Amico 1936, 7, nn. 10–11.

these humble theatre figures to entrust them, calling them to act by their side, to the court jesters, servants who, blessed with a ready spirit, with jocular character and a certain salacity, had in addition to the job of serving their masters also that of entertaining them" (1981, 10).

In short order, according to Pepe, these jesters (the word he uses also means "buffoons") discovered that their new work attracted more attention than the text itself. They discovered, in a word, acting—a discovery that set them free, since "they could refuse to remain in slavery to the palace, depart for the piazzas, live a free life, offering to the crowds that frequented the fairs and markets some samples of this skill. They realized that this new experience gained at the palace could become an authentic profession that could allow them to live without binding them to slavery" (1981, 10).[5]

Chapter 2, "The First Mask," expands upon the thesis just stated. The jesters, liberated from palace service by means of acting, "recited from improvised platforms called *banchi* during the spring, summer, and autumn in the piazza and in taverns during the winter" (1981, 12).[6] More important than the stage itself is the fact that these jesters at first worked solo. "Troupes did not exist, nor duets, nor trios. Every 'jester-actor' was alone in front of his audience."[7] Alone, the jester-turned-actor recited "extracts from comedies learned by rote when he recited at court, monologues he himself wrote, pieces that he improvised on the spot. Neither literary form nor good style had importance. Theatricality counted. Theatrically, even today, a speech imperfect from a literary point of view but delivered with spontaneity is more valued than one perfect in terms of literature but which becomes arid and cold in the speaker's mouth" (1981, 12).

Here again, Pepe plants a few words about language, especially the use of Venetian dialect by these proto-*commedianti*, but he soon leaves that subject in favor of a discussion of costume and mask: "Almost all of the 'jester-actors' dressed in the same style: a short tunic of coarse cloth fastened at the waist by a cord, wide pantaloons of the same fabric, on the head a white felt cap like that of the Goliards, with two peacock's feathers in back. On the face a coarse *papier-mâché* mask with a large

---

[5]Pepe does not elaborate as to how the servants obtained their freedom.

[6]While *banchi* literally means "benches," it also can be translated "counters" or even "street stalls," and can refer both to a temporary stage, as Pepe uses it here, and to the benches on which spectators might sit, though no evidence exists for a seated audience in the present context.

[7]Although *compagnia* most easily becomes "company" in English, I prefer the term "troupe" as a translation more suited to the *commedia* environment.

eagle-beak nose. Only the color of the mask—some red, some yellow, some green—distinguished one from another. In fact, even the name was the same for all: *Zanni*" (1981, 15).

This name, *Zanni*, weaves its way through the whole warp and woof of the *commedia dell'arte* tapestry. Numerous scholars, several of them cited by Pepe in this chapter, have pondered its origin, its meaning, its significance. Pepe begins his discussion of this topic by stating that "the *Zanni* began as a caricature of the poor, ignorant peasant from the Bergamo valleys (and his original language was precisely that of the Brembana Valley), plunging into the city to seek work as a servant or a porter" (1981, 19). After refusing to be drawn into the argument over the possible Atellan heritage of this character (noting in an uncharacteristically terse sentence that "precise references are lacking" [1981, 20]), and only skimming the topic of the derivation of the name itself, Pepe closes this chapter by noting that each performer did distinguish himself by adding "to the name *Zanni* his own artistic name—this being a sign of conceited aspiration to a proprietary personality—resulting in: *Zan Capella, Zan Farina, Zan Battocchio, Zan Gurgolo, Zan Falopa, Zan Fritata, Zan Gradela*, and so on" (1981, 20).[8] With their spelling adjusted to modern Italian, most of these surnames take on actual meanings: *Capella* (usually spelled *cappella*) denotes either a chapel or, and this seems more appropriately suggestive, the head of a mushroom; *Farina* is flour; *Battocchio* signifies the clapper of a bell (albeit with one "t" instead of two); *Gurgolo*, probably a derivative of *gorgoglio*, means gurgle or gurgling; a *faloppa* is a defective cocoon, and a *fallo* is a phallus; a *frittata* is an omelet while "making an omelet" (*fare una frittata*) means idiomatically making a mess out of something; *Gradela* could derive from *gradevole*, pleasant. These jester-*zanni* must have had trouble reciting with their tongues planted so firmly in their cheeks.

Chapter 3, "Arlecchino, Brighella, and Il Magnifico," pursues the progress from *zanni* to the actual *commedia* masks. The alteration became both necessary and logical when *zanni* started working in pairs. "The first recounted the stories, quaint to bizarre ones from the repertoire, the second comically annotated them with *lazzi*, quips, winks, in one rippling game of comic spirit" (1981, 21). As one might expect, a pair of *zanni* also discovered the need to dress differently, shedding the ubiq-

---

[8]In regard to the name itself, Pepe cites the possibility that it originated with Gian Andrea Cimador, a performer from Ferrara who "as a comedian had called himself *Zanni*, a derivation of Gianni," and that other performers started using the name after observing his success. Cimador's birth date is obscure, but he died in 1684.

uitous, burlap-like outfit described above in favor of individualized costumes that suited the nature of their respective identities:

> The *First Zanni,* more restrained in the stage game than the second, less dynamic in gesture, less capricious, less mimic, added green frogs to the white tunic, and on his shoulders a short green mantle; decorated his pants with lateral green hands; on his feet wore white shoes with green pompoms and a green pompom also on his white beret. He no longer wore the grotesque mask of colored *papier mâché* but a half-mask of beaten leather, brown in color, with the expression of a frowning cat, not sleeping, on the alert. Thus transformed, the *Primo Zanni* in addition to costume changed even his name and assumed that of *Brighella.*
>
> No less his stage companion who, having to represent because of his constitutional character a down-at-the-heels servant, eccentric and penniless, always starving, to demonstrate this stubborn misery covered his costume with multicolored patches which, placed one next to the other, in a tasteful game of pink, green, and yellow tints, gave to the costume an unexpected, festive harmony. On his feet black shoe-socks over white stockings; at his waist a belt into which was inserted a paddle to defend himself (forced as he was to sleep under bridges, having neither a house nor a hovel that might accommodate him) from the gangs that roamed around at night; on his head he placed a sugar-loaf felt cap, which he transformed according to the situation in which his personality found itself, making it haughty if the folds were thrown to the side, tearful if the folds fell over his eyes, defiant if placed the other way. . . . On his face he also, like his companion *Brighella,* placed a brown-colored half-mask of beaten leather, this also with the characteristic little face of a cat, but with an expression charmingly and cunningly sweet, with a red pimple over the right eyebrow's curve. At first this character wore a beard and as a name assumed that of *Truffaldino,* sanguine and fleshly in contrast to his pusillanimity, almost to underline the obvious even more. (1981, 21–22)

Minus the beard, and with a black mask rather than a brown, this mask became *Arlecchino* after a period of being called by either name, as well as numerous others.[9] Like the classical Athenians before them, the *zanni* could not content themselves with a pair of characters. After "repeating the game continually and with few variations, the comedians, sensing the weariness that it must have caused the spectators, enlarged its capacity, inserting into the duet a third character, called the old man of comedy" (1981, 30). This third cast member was not *Pantalone,* or at least not yet. Rather, he bore the name *Magnifico,* meaning the lord or master. In all but name he was *Pantalone,* as Pepe's description of his costume clearly

---

[9]Pepe cites twenty-two examples, a multiplicity that to me nominates this *Second Zanni* as the true heir of the *zanni* identity and spirit.

indicates: "red jerkin, with red pants like long underwear that ended in red shoes. On his shoulders a long, black cloak *(Zimmara)*, on his chin a long, pointed beard and his face half-concealed by a black half-mask with a hooked nose, on his head a black beret over white, escaping hair" (1981, 30). This costume changed slightly but significantly after *Magnifico* became *Pantalaone*, to reveal a "red jerkin (or jacket); short trousers of the same color and fabric as the jerkin, stopping at the knee; red socks and, on the feet, black Turkish slippers or black cloth shoes. On his head . . . a beret of black cloth to cover his long white hair, at his waist a black belt to which is hooked the purse that holds his money. On his face he wears the black half-mask with large white eyebrows and a hooked nose. On his chin a pointed beard of the same color hair, a beard always in motion to emphasize the tremors of age and the eternal grumbling of the old merchant. On his shoulders a long black coat" (1981, 35).

A side-by-side, head-to-toe comparison makes the differences clearer:

Magnifico	*Pantalone*
black beret or red toque[10]	black beret
white hair	white hair
black half-mask with hooked nose	black half-mask with bushy, white eyebrows and hooked nose
white, pointed beard	white, pointed beard
long, black or red coat *(Zimmara)*	long, black *Zimmara*
red jerkin	red jerkin or jacket
	black belt with money pouch attached
red pants like long underwear	knee-length, black breeches
	red socks
red shoes	black Turkish slippers or cloth shoes

Although Pepe does not explain the reason for the alteration in the mask's personality, he does describe the characteristics of each of its two stages. Starting as "the old man of comedy . . . a rustic farmer, an introvert, miserly, anything but entertaining," the first version, "was suddenly transformed into the *Magnifico*, the mask of the old Venetian merchant. . . . Often he assumed the habit of the Doge's advisor." Pepe further characterizes him as "a foul old man, depraved, miserly, enemy of the young but not the young to whom, libidinous as he is, he pays

---

[10]Pepe mentions the red toque and red *zimmara* as variations on page 35.

relentless court" (1981, 30). *Pantalone,* on the other hand, embodies "a more dignified personage, comic but not ridiculous and clownish like his predecessor, even though he retains the former's avarice and that amorous fancy surely not consonant with his age" (1981, 35). Moreover, *Pantalone* is, according to Andrea Perrucci, "a mature person, who makes himself ridiculous in that, while he ought to be a person of authority and good example and a warning to others, he, cultivated by love, behaves like a child" (1981, 35).[11] Pepe further defines this mask by citing Pier Maria Cecchini's description of *Pantalone* as "a serious role but mixed, however, with ridicule in language and dress. He who plays him, however, ought to retain that portion of gravity that is never detached from his personality, which ought to reprimand, persuade, command, advise, and do the thousand other offices of an ingenious man."[12]

We are now in chapter 4, which bears the same title as the book itself. Pepe here launches a brief discussion of Allardyce Nicoll's analysis of Renaissance illustrations of *Pantalone,* which picture him "with muscular thighs and members of which any athlete might be jealous."[13] This virile imagery, according to Pepe, more accurately depicts the true *Pantalone* than have many early-modern interpreters of the mask. Actors of the sixteenth and seventeenth centuries, he complains, too often opted for a more readily ridiculous, tottering senility, a tendency that unfortunately often persists today: "The image of a *Pantalone* thus conceived is thus no longer that of *Pantalone* as seen in the Renaissance (when old man did not necessarily mean a man on the edge of the grave) but the sum of the two personalities, the fusion of two masks in one: *Magnifico* and *Pantalone,* drawing, in spite of the lessons of Perrucci and Cecchini, a figure eminently and exclusively comic" (1981, 44–45).

That *Pantalone* is not exclusively comic is a theme sounded frequently in the book. For the present, Pepe drops it as quickly as he had picked it up and turns instead to the matter of *Pantalone's* name and its possible origin: "The suppositions are many, some even quite risky. Two seem the most logically acceptable to me: that which says that the name of *Pantalone* is simply derived from San Pantaleone, patron of the city of Venice, and the other, which attracts me more, that has the name of the

---

[11]Pepe is quoting from Perrucci n.p.

[12]Cited on page 37 without reference to any specific title. In note 8, page 6, Pepe identifies Cecchini, born in 1563, as the well-educated scion of a family of Ferrarese actors. He provides the title of the work presumably quoted here in note 20, page 25. See Cecchini 1678.

[13]Pepe notes Nicoll as the author of *History of English Drama 1600–1900,* but does not specifically identify the source of this analysis. It is *The World of Harlequin,* 1963, 49.

Venetian mask derived from the motto *pianta-leone* [planter of lions], as the Venetian merchants were commonly called for their habit of erecting a Lion of St. Mark on a column (planting the column with the Lion on top) in every newly-acquired territory" (1981, 46).

Chapter 5, "The First *Pantalone*," contains an extended examination of the question indicated in its title. In the process, Pepe introduces additional material dealing with the early history of *commedia dell'arte*. He cites both the "first official document that attests to the establishment of a troupe of professional actors," a notary deed drawn up in 1545, and a 1530 letter that clearly establishes the existence of professional troupes at the time of its writing (1981, 47).[14]

As to the first portrayer of *Pantalone*, Pepe opens the dispute by noting that Franca Angelini, in the *Enciclopedia dello spettacolo*, Giacomo Oreglia, in an unnamed "essay on the *commedia dell'arte* published at Stockholm in 1961," and Silvio D'Amico, in *Teatro italiano*, credited this honor to Giulio Pasquati, a Paduan actor who eventually became a member of *I Gelosi* (1981, 49).[15] Pepe then offers his own candidate, a Venetian actor named Andrea Calmo. Using a published collection of Calmo's letters as his source, Pepe delineates the actor's biography in some detail, especially in regard to establishing that Calmo was already playing a fully delineated *Pantalone* in advance of Pasquati's career (Rossi 1888). Calmo started in theatre as a playwright, and Pepe notes that he created old man roles that "carry in themselves the characteristics of the mask [of *Pantalone*]," especially a character from Calmo's 1553 *La Rodiana* [*The Girl from Rhodes*]. At the close of this chapter, Pepe establishes an imaginative, hypothetical link between Calmo and Pasquati: "This Calmo traveled frequently, with his company, to give shows in the vicinity of Padua and there, as a student, the young Giulio Pasquati, who would be passionately fond of it, had certainly intended to act the mask of *Pantalone*. He who impassioned him might have been the incentive that made him abandon his studies and set off toward the exercise of the

---

[14]The deed, for which Pepe provides only a vague reference to Mario Apollonio's *Storia del Teatro Italiano* (*History of Italian Theatre*), named a Paduan actor and author, Ser Maffio de Re, as the troupe's leader. Federico Doglio quotes the entire document (1989, 2:186–87). Another Paduan author-actor, Angelo Beolco, better known as Ruzzante, wrote the 1530 letter to the Duke of Ferrara, regretting that he could not find enough professional actors in Padua "to constitute the staff of a worthy troupe." The Duke had invited Ruzzante to form such a group and bring it to Ferrara. Here, Pepe cites Zorzi 1967 without giving a page number.

[15]Pepe gives a precise reference only from the *Enciclopedia dello Spettacolo* (1960, 7:1727). He cites D'Amico 1936 without a page reference and provides no further information about Oreglia's essay.

dramatic art" (1981, 56). While this possibility has its attractions, they are not well enough documented here to transform them into credible fact.

In the sixth and final chapter of the first part of his book, "*Pantalone's* Language" (Il Linguaggio di *Pantalone*), Pepe offers a number of quotations from the mask's repertoire of "premeditated passages," which include "maxims, proverbs, proverbial phrases" and downright rants and curses (1981, 60).[16] All of these make use of *Pantalone's* characteristic Venetian dialect and their length places them beyond inclusion in this brief article. I will, however, include Pepe's comment on the general tenor of this mask's speech: "It is certain that this mask knows how to use in an admirable manner, with diverting satisfaction, all the gradations of the Venetian tongue, both when he wants to derive comic effects from that language and when comedy turns serious in his threats, in his curses; against servants, his son, and the women who play jokes on him, he uses terms of low vulgarity" (1981, 60).

As his final comment on *Pantalone's* colorful, individualized rhetoric, Pepe refers to it as "a very well-marked track to direct the interpretation of a character." It is language, then, combined with situations of particular types, that circumscribes and determines the mask's "type." Having used this word, Pepe delivers a parting shot aimed squarely at Carlo Goldoni: "Later, Goldoni would make a *character* of it [the type], humanizing it. Because of this, when *Pantalone* is gallant in Goldoni's plays he is so without that absurdity that characterizes him in the *commedia dell'arte* and he is more generous than avaricious. A character, Bragaglia would say, travestied from *Pantalone*, no longer bound to the conventions of the *scenarios*; on the contrary, a willful alteration of the original type, which would be exasperated even further in this alteration when Goldoni took *Pantalone's* mask away and left him with his beard but with a bare face" (1981, 64).

At this point, "at the comedy of character in which, for the masks, there is no longer any room," Pepe closes his historical account. "The nineteenth century and the romantic theatre are at the gates" (1981, 64).

Despite the impressive range of sources he uses to support it, Pepe's account of *Pantalone* in particular and *commedia dell'arte* in general often has the ring of rationalization about it. We have, in this modern *commediante*, not an objective and dispassionate historian but a subjective and impassioned performer who has sought to forge the available facts into a

---

[16]*Brani premeditati* stand in contrast to dialogue *all'improvviso* or *a soggetto*, the latter best translated "ad-lib."

coherent and logical plot line. Where the historian's shoulders might show with a shrug the impossibility of a factual connection between points A and B, Pepe, with a point of Pantalone's beard, adroitly leaps the chasm and bridges the two sides with a usually plausible conjecture.

Should this leap seem a case of a fool rushing in where angels fear to tread, remember that *commedia* masks originated as *buffoni* and that the *commedia* never had much patience with angels. If one chooses to winnow away the chaff, good kernels of knowledge will still remain.

Works Cited

Cecchini, Pier Maria. *Frutti delle moderne Commedie e avvisi a chi le recite* (Fruits of the Modern Comedies and Advice to Those Who Act Them). Padua: at its author's expense, 1678.

D'Amico, Silvio. *Teatro italiano*. Milan: Bompiani, 1936.

Doglio, Federico. *Teatro in Europa*. Milan: Garzanti, 1989.

Enciclopedia dello spettacolo. Rome: Casa editrice Le Maschere, 1960.

Nicoll, Allardyce. *The World of Harlequin*. London: Cambridge University Press, 1963.

Pandolfi, Vito. *Il teatro di Rinascimento e la Commedia dell'Arte* (Renaissance Theatre and the *Commedia dell'Arte*). Rome: Lerici Editore, 1969.

Pepe, Nico. *Pantalone: storia di una maschera e di un attore*. Udine: Grafiche Tirelli, 1981.

Perrucci, A. *Dell'arte rappresentativa premeditata ed all'improvviso* (The Skill of Premeditated and Improvised Performance). Florence: Sansoni Antiquariato, 1961.

Rossi, Vittorio. *Le lettere di messer Andrea Calmo*. Turin: Ermanno Loescher, 1888.

Zorzi, L. *Ruzzante*. Turin: Einaudi, 1967.

Commedia at Coney Island

Christopher C. Newton

N NEW YORK's Little Italy on April 14, 1903, an example of one of
the more curious legacies of the *commedia dell'arte* tradition was
performed. The production, *Pulcinella candidato democratico con Farfariello impazzito per la tragedia* (Pulcinella Democratic candidate with
Farfariello crazy about tragedy; Aleandri 1984, 166 and Appendix VIII),
suggests by its title the convoluted mix of Old and New World characters,
forms, and language. This two-act vehicle for the best-known Italian-
American comic of the period, Eduardo Migliaccio, is one of many titular
examples of the hybrid pollination of *commedia dell'arte* in America. No
doubt other forms such as *teatro varietà, teatri a sezioni, basso popolo,* dialect
theatre, minstrel shows, and vaudeville influenced the creation of Migliaccio's unique Italian-American drama type, but the legacy of *commedia dell'arte* is unmistakable. A sampling of some of the other 300 titles
in the repertoire reinforces the image of an ingenious dramatic alchemist:
Migliaccio lampoons an American politician in *Pulcinello Sindaco di Chicago* (Pulcinello Mayor of Chicago); he presents a version of the *commedia "Il Capitano"* character in *Il Cafone Patrioto* (The Italian Patriot);
and in *Iammo a Cunnailando* (Let's Go to Coney Island), Migliaccio's
multiple-personality character creation, "Farfariello," does his best to
lure the object of his desire, a "sprinche-chik," away from her watchful
parents and into the "Luppo-Luppo" ride of Coney Island (Aleandri
1984, 455–81). Eclectic in its sources, Migliaccio's drama became na-
tionally popular among Italian-Americans by the time of the First World
War.

The creative output of Eduardo Migliaccio tells only part of the story;

the particular biographical dynamics of this immigrant artist reflect powerfully in the creation of a new drama. Migliaccio began his career modeling himself on *Il Dottore, Stenterello,* and especially the Neapolitan *Pulcinella,* but as he became familiar with the unique tastes of immigrants, he expanded his vision to include the Italian-American milieu familiar to audiences from San Francisco's North Beach to Boston's North End. The issue of the drama gradually changed emphasis from a grasp on the Old World to an entertaining encounter with the New. Perhaps the most revealing testament to his craft was the invitation to and triumphant tour of Italy after World War I. Though Migliaccio was knighted in Italy, there was no doubt in his mind that he would return to America, where he had found fertile ground for his unique version of *commedia dell'arte.* One should issue a caveat when applying the term *commedia dell'arte* to cover a broad historical period, for the Pulcinella of 1900 or the Farfariello of 1920 is not the same as the Pulcinella of Silvio Fiorelli, 200 years before. Of course the *commedia dell'arte* tradition was not reborn pristine and immutable in America after the decline of the lineage in France and Italy, but rather elements of the *commedia dell'arte* found new purpose in the hands of a skilled performer, and the dramatization of the immigrant experience brought life to an old tradition.

The Development of the Artist

At the height of his popularity in 1919, Eduardo Migliaccio was featured by the noted theatre critic Carl Van Vechten in a *Theatre Magazine* spotlight. Van Vechten remarked on how involved and meticulous the now well-paid Migliaccio was in maintaining and developing his craft. Migliaccio himself still made his own masks, his sister made the costumes, and his son acted as dresser. Most remarkable to Van Vechten was that Farfariello made "his own wigs. This last detail amazed me when I learned of it. It would seem that Farfariello, without perhaps having heard of Gordon Craig, is exactly following out Craig's idea of the artist of the theatre who is to be and do everything" (1919, 34). The mention of Gordon Craig is significant. Van Vechten's suggestion that the creation of Farfariello might be a model for the modern theatre of the early twentieth century highlights the importance of Migliaccio as a pivotal artist. Van Vechten astutely observed that Migliaccio's artistic simplicity and self-reliance was a living example of some of Craig's ideas (see Fisher 1988, 245–75). And though the comparison of Craig's ideas and Migliaccio's *commedia* practice was intriguing to Van Vechten, surely practical performance considerations guided the artist while theoretical assessment came as an afterthought. Even so, Migliaccio's first encounter with the *commedia dell'arte* tradition occurred not with professional intentions in New York, but rather with boyhood enthusiasm in his native Naples at the Teatro Nuovo.

Eduardo Migliaccio was born in Salerno, just outside Naples, in 1882 (Aleandri 1984, 130).[1] Unlike many other southern Italians who emigrated to America, Migliaccio came from a wealthy urban family. As a young boy he was enrolled in the Instituto Belle Arti in Naples where he studied design and plastic arts by day and attended the theatre at night. The famous Pulcinella Teatro San Carlino had recently closed (1884), but much of the repertoire was still being performed along with French farces at the Teatro Nuovo (MacClintock 1920, 70). One of the greatest early influences appears to have been the *macchiettista,* Nicolo Maldaceo. And though Migliaccio was not a *figlio dell'arte,* born into a *commedia* troupe and thus trained through inheritance, his natural aptitude was fostered by factors that would serve as an effective theatrical apprenticeship. His upbringing was atypical of the majority of the people of the Risorgimento, who would eventually become his audience in the New World. Because of his family's wealth, Migliaccio was given the leisure to become well versed in Italian Renaissance literature. The technical school of design and plastic arts would later be invaluable in the physical creation of Farfariello's drama. Finally, Migliaccio's attendance at the Pulcinella theatre as a youth provided him with an important model for his future creative energy.

In 1897 Migliaccio took his worldly goods, including three books on Pulcinella performance, and joined his father who was working in a bank in Hazelton, Pennsylvania.[2] Though Migliaccio was miserable in his job and longed to move to New York City, the work as a client correspondent contributed to the development of a modern *commedia* artist with a social work slant. Migliaccio's banking duties included writing letters to the families of illiterate Italian miners. The bank transferred money and news across the Atlantic, and though Migliaccio no doubt felt the job was beneath someone trained in the arts, he did occasionally get creative enough with his surrogate letter-writing to find himself in trouble with the bank's clients. Within a year Migliaccio had complained so much about being stuck in Hazelton that his father arranged for a similar job for him in Little Italy, New York.

The new job was no more interesting, but it did afford more free time.

---

[1]Biographical data are taken mostly from Aleandri, as opposed to often apocryphal accounts in other sources.

[2]Aleandri (1984, 131) puts the date of Migliaccio's immigration to the United States in 1897; Lawrence Estavan (1991, 55) lists Migliaccio's first arrival in 1895.

Migliaccio, inspired by the model of the Teatro Nuovo, used the extra time to write sketches and songs. Success, however, was not instant. His first career attempt—as an interlude act for a marionette performance of *Orlando Furioso*—was disastrous. The young Migliaccio was incensed when the puppets got more applause than he did, and when he tried to save his performance with continued improvisation, his efforts were met with a flying soda bottle from the audience. The next attempt at the *caffe-concerto*, La Villa Napoli, met with greater appreciation. There Migliaccio tempered his material for the specific crowd. A more traditional presentation of Neapolitan songs with a little bit of physical narration thrown in was exactly what the cafe crowd wanted. *Femmene-Fe* became his first big hit and the source of his stage name.[3] By 1900, Farfariello was the main attraction at the Cafe Pennachio, and he made the important transition from amateur to professional performer. With a strong local following, a catchy stage name, and a growing repertoire, Farfariello felt secure enough once again to improvise and experiment with new dramatic material and forms.

The Creation of an Effective Form

The *commedia dell'arte* character of Pulcinella in late nineteenth-century Italy as well as in turn-of-the-century Little Italy productions was used increasingly as a vehicle for topical comedy in an otherwise unrelated play. Though Pulcinella continued to be written into original plays and adaptations, he was rarely necessary to the plot. The freedom of this character to move through any kind of play gave considerable flexibility to the design of an evening's entertainment. Considering the broad range of offerings in many theatres (the bill of fare would likely include several musical solos, duets, a dramatic tragedy, an operetta, a farce, and a host of comic interludes), it is not surprising that Pulcinella or the Florentine Stenterello might appear in a variety of contexts. For Farfariello, this flexibility enabled the little butterfly to appear in full-length plays, in musical revues, or by himself in a *macchietta* character sketch. The freedom of Pulcinella to appear in any number of theatrical settings also had its disadvantages, especially in the immigrant community. Farfariello found that the tradional material successful in Naples

---

[3]"Farfariello" literally means the "little butterfly," but it also plays on the secondary meanings and derivations of the word. Vladimiro Macchi (1988, 1616) gives the second meaning of "Farfalla" as a "fickle (flighty, inconstant) person, flibbertigibbet," and "Farfallone" suggests "dandy, fop, philanderer." These descriptive synonyms reflect the *commedia* tradition and anticipate the nature of Farfariello's performance.

was becoming less effective with residents of the "melting pot." The effective local allusions were no longer Italian, but American, and the sheer variety of human types encountered in immigrant ghettos suggested that the *commedia dell'arte* tradition needed a larger repertoire. In 1900, during the period of heavy Italian migration, the frames of reference of the immigrant and his *contadini* back home were relatively similar, but as Italian-Americans settled and interacted with their new environment, the context of their world changed. Sociologists Primeggia and Varacalli have broadly traced the flow of southern Italian humor into America: "An Italian might enjoy a Pulcinella farce in Naples before embarking for the United States. Upon arriving in New York City, after leaving Ellis Island, the newcomer could see a performance of the same Pulcinella adventure in a number of theatres or cafes in Little Italy. Later, immigrant humor experienced a transformation and came to focus on the Italian adjusting to American life" (1990, 47). The dynamic that Farfariello began to understand as a bank correspondent now was fully realized in his unique creation of the *macchietta coloniale*.

The *macchietta coloniale* was a simple scene that dramatized the conflicts suffered by an immigrant type. Sometimes the character would be placed in a larger comedy, but frequently the performance was done as a monologue. The premise of the *macchietta* was often not unlike the traditional *lazzi* with a scheme to meet the girl behind her husband's (or parent's back), or a device to outfox a thief. The most significant development was the new malleability of the performer's identity. The subliminal crafty identity of the performer, Farfariello, remained behind the depictions of immigrant characters, but increasingly the performance became a pastiche of immigrant life rather than the presentational wit of Pulcinella.

Migliaccio's expansion of the *commedia dell'arte* to *macchietta coloniale* appeared also to have joined two disparate aesthetic perspectives. Reviews of the performances frequently praised both the realism and the *commedia* tradition of Farfariello. When the *macchiette coloniale* were done in San Francisco the reaction was the following: "Farfariello was modern, but he was also the product of a long evolution"; and, "If Farfariello is 'up to the minute' in his sketches from New York life there is something about the technique of his art that suggests a century of tradition as its basis. It is medieval in its realistic satire and its essentially robust comedy. Rather than to characterize it as realistic, however, one should say that it is caricature based on close observation of the actual" (Estavan 1991, 56). But a New York reviewer was willing to consider Farfariello's five stages of *The Drunk* close enough to true realism that it should be considered as valuable medical information on alcoholism

(Parker 1914). The label "realism" must of course be used with caution, for it should be remembered that all of Farfariello's depictions included extreme makeup effects and padded costumes; half of the *macchiette* incorporated masks, and at least a third of his pieces involved a song. The genius of Farfariello was in the recognition and use of the dramatic truths crystallized by the *commedia dell'arte* tradition within a recognizable context for a modern audience.

The Expansion of Traditional Characters

The wealth of iconographic depictions of *commedia dell'arte* character types dominates the pages of theatre history books. Indeed the visual image created by these depictions suggests a society of performers in exaggerated poses who rely heavily on the distinctions of their costumes and masks to convey a dramatic message. Though there appears to be a dress code for performers engaged in presenting a traditional character type, variety (within boundaries) seems to be more the rule than dramatic cloning. Variety is especially appropriate when describing Pulcinella. Duchartre in *The Italian Comedy* begins his chapter on the *commedia dell'arte* figure of Pulcinella by highlighting the spectrum of potential Pulcinellas: "The doom of duality was pronounced against Pulcinella even before he was born, for he had, it appears, the special privilege of having two fathers, Maccus and Bucco. Inasmuch as Maccus and Bucco were not in the least alike, Pulcinella was always drawn toward opposite poles by his dual heredity" (1966, 208). According to Duchartre, the various incarnations of the Pulcinella in the sixteenth and seventeenth centuries included coarse bumpkin, magistrate, poet, valet, bachelor, thief, boastful coward, Neapolitan ruffian, and a French officer. By the nineteenth century, the Pulcinella derivative was portrayed from one end of the spectrum to the other, as a bumpkin coward afraid of Vesuvius or as a generous servant scheming successfully for a Christmas Day feast. When Migliaccio reconstituted the *commedia dell'arte* Pulcinella into the *macchietta coloniale* of Farfariello in the Little Italy of 1900, the break with Old World traditions was effectively more gradual and evolutionary than might initially appear by the change in nomenclature.

The characters that had made up the various Pulcinellas continued in American forms. The braggart soldier and the bounding bachelor, already mentioned above, fit nicely in the traditional repertoire with *'O Cafone c'a Sciamerica* (The Country Bumpkin in a Tuxedo), *L'imbroglione* (The Swindler), *Il Cafone furbo* (The Shrewd Country Bumpkin), and *The Judge* (Aleandri 1984, 455–70). The more traditional figures were doubtless familiar to the American audience recently arrived from Italy, but certainly the real interest of the immigrant audience must have been stirred by the transitional character creations of Farfariello. The *macchietta* titled *Un Vecchio emigrato siciliano* (An Old Sicilian Immigrant), *L'elegante napoletano capitato in America* (The Elegant Neapolitan Who Finds Himself in America), and *Il borsaiouolo coloniale italo-americano* (The Italian-American Pickpocket) (Aleandri 1984, 455–70) afford generous proof of Farfariello's familiarity with the immigrant population. Farfariello was also an accomplished impersonator of female characters and *Rosi Spaghetti: il tipo della cafoncella italiana americanizzata* (The Type of Italian Countrygirl Who Has Become Americanized) attests to his development of a wide spectrum of immigrant types. Indeed, Farfariello was not afraid of depicting political types or celebrities, as in the performances of *La Suffragetta, Il Divo, Caruso,* and *Il Rosso* (The Red, based on Riccardo Cordiffero; Aleandri 1984, 455–70). Most pieces were not concerned with radical subjects, but more focused on finding the humor in the confusion of meeting a new culture. The core of human frailty important to the *commedia dell'arte* characters was by the process of adoption of immigrant types strengthened, and the departure from tradition reimbursed the altered drama with greatly increased character depth.

Some of the recorded lines of *O figlio d'o cafone che raggione* (The Son of the Thinking Greenhorn) reveal the bittersweet nature of the humor: "Today in this land here the American man is in charge and he can do anything he wants to you; therefore when he sees an Italian, even if he were a king, they would call him a dago! I say for what reason, do you offend Italians? . . . Because though I am a greenhorn, I have countrymen who are masters of science, your teachers, who can make for you, anything you can dream of! . . . What Americans do here not even pigs do where I come from: they blow their noses with their hands right in the street . . . and we are ghinnys?@!: With tobacco in their mouths they eat lunch . . . a drunken woman you find on every corner" (Aleandri 1984, 468–69). Naturally the pantomimic depiction of these American types would have carried the bulk of the humor, but it is important to reflect that the *macchietta coloniale* was not all hot-foot and pants-dropping.

Certainly the tradition of improvisation allowed the Old World *commedia dell'arte* to address and satirize local conditions and figures. Not a great deal of proof exists, however, that *commedia* performers made this satire a consistent practice. The collected sketches of Farfariello do provide a valuable source for the possibilities of not only the great variety of character permutations, but also the potential for an expanded use of *commedia dell'arte* humor into social satire for a modern audience.

The Importance of a New Immigrant Language

In any discussion of the *commedia dell'arte* tradition, it is essential to comment on the physical presentation of the performance. If recent recreations of *commedia dell'arte* style productions are any guide, then one would expect a highly physically capable performer, with the agility of a gymnast and the precision of a mime. Descriptions of Renaissance *commedia dell'arte* acting styles are scant and not complete enough to render a confident illustration, but if the method of Farfariello is to serve as any guide to the link between the modern era and the Pulcinella theatre of the Teatro Nuovo, then the weight of emphasis would come down on the side of precise gestures rather than on broad slapstick and tumbling. Farfariello kept the scale of his performance small (most of the cafe stages could hardly accommodate more than three actors at best), and the rehearsal hall was confined to the full-length mirror at home. Alma Migliaccio, Eduardo's daughter, remembers her father "rehearsing long hours before a mirror, [he] precisely planned and executed every gesture, dance step, line delivery, [and] vocal inflection" (Sogliuzzo 1973, 69). Indeed, Farfariello made enough of a science out of his precise physical work that he became the subject of an anthropological study at Columbia University on "Characteristic and Symbolic Gestures among Italians" (Efron 1934). Despite the windmilling stereotype of expressive Italians, the photographic evidence of Farfariello presenting posed examples of his characters indicates a precise rather than histrionic approach to posture, expression, and gesture (Migliaccio Collection). Compared to photographs of tragedians Irving, Duse, or Bernhart, the presentation of Farfariello's characters seems sober. The proximity of performer and audience and the sensitivity with which Italians read physical cues (if the Columbia investigation is accurate) encourage the notion that economy and precision with physical movement were most important to the immigrant audience.

The aural element of the performance should not be overlooked, for a similar precision and perhaps even greater complexity surround this element of the *commedia dell'arte*. Gianrenzo Clivio writes compellingly in his article, "The Languages of *Commedia dell'Arte*" about the importance of linguistic codes in *commedia* (1989, 209). The dramatic role of multilingualism could and did play a part in character development throughout the *commedia*'s history, in which different characters command different dialects. Linguistic confusion could also serve as a central plot device not only for the Italian *commedia dell'arte*, but also for the *macchiette* of Farfariello. Farfariello makes great fun of the confusion between "sabre" and "shovel" in a piece depicting the lowly status of the "pick and shovel greenhorno" (Aleandri and Seller 1983, 266). "La Sciabola" is the term for sword among the nobility in Italy, but in the Italian-American vernacular it becomes the label for "shovel." The double entendre of the nobility's mighty weapon and the immigrant ditch-digger's crutch has endless humorous possibilities.

Perhaps the most significant proof of the hybrid process is the use of Italo-American English. *Iammo a Cunnailando* with its hybrid title and sprinkling of Anglicized terms has already been mentioned. Though Farfariello always performed in Italian, he carefully selected and annotated his new English words for dramatic effect. The inclusion of Italglish served at least two new purposes for the *macchietta coloniale*. First, the bastard words became an in-joke, accessible only to the immigrant audience. While the majority of the message was carried in Italian (frequently dialect), the occasional use of American code afforded a knowing superiority over both the naive folk just off the boat and the seemingly all-powerful, previously assimilated American. Secondly, the clumsy-sounding English words, when wedged within a flowing Italian sentence, could easily reflect the discomfort that immigrants felt toward a described American institution. Some of Farfariello's *macchiette* revolved around the entire question of having to adopt a new language.

The following *macchietta* serves as an excellent example, *La lingua 'taliana*. The piece begins with an eight-line prologue leading into the first two verses of a song; then follows a spoken narrative, and the finale is the last verse of the song. The prologue and song's first verse describe the beauty of the Italian language, and the absurd demands in incomprehensible English that an American judge makes on Farfariello who is trying to obtain his citizenship papers. ("It's been twenty years since I came directly here, from my country . . . and yet I haven't yet learned even half a word of English.") The second verse introduces the termagant wife who does understand the judge's English and upbraids her dull husband in Italo-American with epithets like "Iu giachesse" (You jackass) and "Ai brecche iu fesse" (I break you face). Farfariello's response is to retreat into a narrative about the old country and how "the American language is a deformed Italian language, turned upside down," and he cites the ridiculous notion of calling *femmene* "uomeni" (or woman)—a word that sounds very much like the Italian for man. He also lists the confusion over "bread" (an important concept for Italian peasants) which sounds like "prete," which is Italian for priest. Serving "bread" (or, the *prete*) at the table suggests an entire new dimension of Catholicism. Finally, the grumbling Farfariello consoles himself with the thought that Americans quickly run out of curses and that Italians have a thousand at the tips of both their tongues and fingers. The closing verse of the song recounts a sticky situation where the protagonist is threatened on the street by an American gang, and a quick use of gesture and primal language conquers the situation. Farfariello's defense from the taunts of the gang is to put his hand ominously behind his back as if he were carrying a weapon. When he is safely distant from the threat, he reveals the ruse and is met with a Bronx cheer. But our hero has the last laugh, "Because I know the sound from far away. It's an ITALIAN CHEER!" (Aleandri 1984, 456–60).

This example of the *macchietta coloniale* reveals the careful blending of important physical gestures and the harmonious use of the immigrant language to generate humor and community solidarity within the "melting pot" environment. The technique of the *commedia dell'arte* sets the foundation for generating the dramatic scene and character (using very focused visual elements of costume, mask, language, and gesture), and the astute human study made by Migliaccio combines art and substance, tradition and the topical, craft and spontaneity, to create a drama vital to the coterie immigrant audience.

Finally, Migliaccio's creation of Farfariello and the *macchietta coloniale* out of the remnants of the *commedia dell'arte* tradition should be put in the context immigrants encounter and "Americanization," for these were the ultimate boundaries of this unique Italian-American form. A most poignant example of Farfariello's use of his art to Americanize the community can be found toward the end of his life. When the large flow of Italian immigration was reduced to a trickle by new restrictive laws in the early twenties, many Italians in America realized that they needed to acclimate to their adopted country actively (and sometimes obviously). The gradual process was relatively comfortable until tensions mounted in the late thirties between the American government and Mussolini's Italy. The declaration of war between Italy and the United States was the last stage in a fundamental change in Italian-American drama. The great question of allegiance arose, and the pragmatic visionary Farfariello led the way with a sketch in 1942 titled, *Il suldate americane*. Though the piece was 90 percent in Italian, the content was 100 percent American. The refrain echoed, "My first duty is to you America, and second to you, my mother" (Migliaccio Collection). No doubt there was some lampooning of the gung-ho soldier, but the message to the audience was clear: the lives of Italian immigrants were indelibly woven into the American fabric. The evolution from Pulcinella to Farfariello, and from *Il patrioto italiano* to *Il suldate americane* suggests the strength and malleability of the *commedia dell'arte* tradition. Sadly enough, in 1946 when Farfariello died, there was no one with the technique and training to carry on performing the *macchietta coloniale* in the Italian-American community. The effort would have likely been useless. The genre had served its purpose and had lost its audience partially because of its own success at helping Italians to Americanize gradually. By 1950 the Italian immigrant theatre in America had all but vanished. For a brief period in the first half of the twentieth century *commedia dell'arte* had revived from its decline since Goldoni and had reconstituted traditional elements into a unique American form. Migliaccio's vehicle of Farfariello, the New World Pulcinella, appealed to a specific need within his audience. However, by the time the forces of television, suburban migration, and Cold War pop culture reached the height of their impact on all Americans, the need for the distinctive Italian-American performance genre correspondingly disappeared. Once again the *commedia dell'arte* is in a largely silent period, but if the durable nature of *commedia dell'arte* history is any guide, it is plausible that Pulcinella and Farfariello will reappear in the future in a new and serviceable medium.

Works Cited

Aleandri, Emelise. "A History of Italian-American Theatre: 1900–1905." Ph.D. diss., City University of New York, 1984.

Aleandri, Emelise, and Maxine Schwartz Seller. "Italian-American Theatre." In *Ethnic Theatre in the United States,* edited by Maxine Schwartz Seller, 237–76. Westport, CT: Greenwood Press, 1983.

Clivio, Gianrenzo. "The Languages of the *commedia dell'arte.*" In *The Science of Buffoonery: Theory and History of the* Commedia dell'Arte, edited by Domenico Pietropaolo, 209–37. Toronto: Dovehouse Editions, 1989.

Duchartre, Pierre Louis. *The Italian Comedy.* Translated by Randolph Weaver. 1929. Reprint. New York: Dover Publications, 1966.

Efron, David. Letter to Eduardo Migliaccio, 1934. Contained in Migliaccio Collection box at the Immigration History Research Center, Minneapolis, MN.

Estavan, Lawrence. *The Italian Theatre in San Francisco.* Edited by Mary A. Burgess. San Bernardino, CA: Borgo Press, 1991.

Fisher, James. "Commedia Iconography in the Theatrical Art of Edward Gordon Craig." In *The* Commedia dell'Arte: *From the Renaissance to Dario Fo,* edited by Christopher Cairns, 245–75. Lewiston, NY: Mellen Press, 1988.

Macchi, Vladimiro. *I Dizionario Sansoni: Italian-English.* 3rd ed. Florence: Sansoni Editore, 1988.

MacClintock, Lander. *The Contemporary Drama of Italy.* Boston: Little Brown and Company, 1920.

Migliaccio Collection box at the Immigration History Research Center, Minneapolis, MN.

Parker, Robert A. "Farfariello, Most Popular Italian Impersonator, Who Scorns

'Big Time' for Ten-Cent Shows." *The New York Press*, January 4, 1914. Clipping in Migliaccio Collection box at the Immigration History Research Center, Minneapolis, MN.

Primeggia, Salvatore, and Joseph A. Varacalli. "Pulcinella to Farfariello to Paone to Cooper to Uncle Floyd: A Socio-Historical Perspective on Southern Italian and Italian-American Comedy." *ECCSSA Journal* no. 1 (1990): 45–51.

Sogliuzzo, Richard. "Notes for a History of the Italian-American Theatre of New York." *Theatre Survey* 14:2 (November 1973): 59–75.

Van Vechten, Carl. "A Night with Farfariello." *Theatre Magazine* 29 (January 1919): 32, 34.

Polichinelle in Paris

Puppetry and the *Commedia dell'Arte*

Jane McMahan

*W*HETHER ONE ACCEPTS the theory that Pulcinella is descended from the character Maccus of the Roman Atellan farces (or an amalgam of Maccus, Bucco, and Docenus) (Nicoll 1963, 65–79), or considers that notion a collective fantasy on the part of eighteenth- and nineteenth-century scholars easily disproven by the paucity of evidence and the likelihood of a character transformation during centuries of change (Smith 1912, 20–26), one glance at the miniature bronze figurine of Maccus discovered in Rome in 1722 (Duchartre 1966, 209) reveals irresistible resemblances. By adopting Anthony Caputi's open-ended approach, tracing a continuity of specific stylistic character traits from antiquity to the Renaissance in "a story of repeated emergences" (1978, 92), we can consider Maccus to be one of the first known embodiments of a comic ideal that has resurfaced over subsequent generations: the germ of a prototype that persists to this day. One such manifestation is the puppet character Polichinelle as curently performed by Philippe Casidanus in Paris. Although differentiated by physical medium and historical context, Casidanus's Polichinelle bears the definitive physical imprint and *esprit* of his predecessor from the *commedia dell'arte*, an earlier manifestation of the malign Maccus prototype. Caputi describes Atellan farce as "a species of short comedy dealing with ordinary life which was developed in Campania in the third century B.C., and later enjoyed such a vogue in republican Rome that it was taken up as a literary form. . . . The form produced . . . characters of tremendous popularity . . . [among them] Bucco, a fool with puffed-out cheeks;

Dossenus, a sharp-witted, rather terrifying hunchback; Maccus, a stupid, awkward fool" (1978, 101).

Certain aspects of the physiognomy of Maccus—the beaked nose, humped back, wide mouth with adjoining circles, sensual lips, spindly legs, malignantly laughing facial expression—reappear in the Neapolitan *commedia* character Pulcinella, the French *commedia* Polichinelle, the French puppet Polichinelle, and the English puppet Punch. Other puppet variants include the Russian Petroushka and the German Kasperle. The character subsumed by all these traditions transmits a common thread of genial blatant knavery.

Pursuing traces of intermediary emergences of this particular comic ideal, Caputi notes the early appearance of a Pulcinella among the retainers of the Carnival King participating in European medieval festivities, folkloric enactments of ritual revels that occurred in preparation for Lent and Easter (1978, 51). Caputi writes, "In southern Italy, Pulcinella was supreme among the carnival demons. His characteristic dress consisted of a black, long-nosed mask, a conical hat, white clothes, and a stick, and he had a distinctively shrill voice thought appropriate to the dead. Like Harlequin and Zanni, he typically led the carnival rout, and in Calabria he frequently was [King] Carnival" (1978, 62–63).

Pulcinella emerges in another popular vein, *La Canzone di Zeza* (D'Aponte 1987, 71–104), a traditional play with oral and literary antecedents dating to perhaps as early as the sixteenth century, that is still performed outside of Naples during carnival time. Here Pulcinella vehemently opposes the marriage of his pregnant daughter but is effectively outwitted by his wife, Zeza.

Tracing the development of Pulcinella from antiquity through the Renaissance, one can point to the omnipresent existence of popular entertainers, among them the traveling mimes who, after their expulsion from the Christian church, may have merged with local entertainers to become the minstrels and jesters of the Middle Ages. A certain bald fool with large ears and a hunchback appeared in the *Comedia Bile,* a fifteenth-century dramatic dialogue, suggesting a possible Pulcinella (Caputi 1978, 91).

The kind of material developed by the plots of the "revue play," a term given by Caputi for the popular Renaissance farces that developed out of the earlier revel play, offered scope for the continued concretization of an emerging character type that would later achieve further definition in the scenarios of the *commedia dell'arte*. A play such as *La farce du Pont aux Anes* (Caputi 1978, 106) features exaggerated physical combat between husband and wife. Numerous European revue plays develop character traits such as stubbornness, intractability, unresponsiveness to discipline, impoliteness, persistent stupidity, obsessive attention to food and sex, and physical deformity. These qualities coalesce in Pulcinella in both the *commedia* and puppet characters. Structural techniques such as deception, transformation, death and revival, undermining of authority figures, madcap pranks, unabated beatings, and repeated surprises are refined in both *commedia* and puppetry to produce a general climate of suspense and unconfined mirth.

The plays of Plautus, modeled perhaps on those of Menander, the plays of the Renaissance humanists such as Grévin, modeled perhaps on the plays of Plautus, and the Ruzzante plays of Beolco were likely to have exerted a seminal influence on later farce traditions, or at least to have shared parallel concerns and motivations while utilizing more elaborate methods. These, along with the popular theatrical traditions outlined above, can in broad terms be considered Pulcinella's heritage, or perhaps, collective unconscious.

Viewed variously by historians, the *commedia* Pulcinella exudes an aura of dizzying diversity. Pierre Louis Duchartre writes: "Pulcinella was never one to be bowed down by the cares and responsibilities of a profession. He was by turns a magistrate, a poet, a master, and a valet, but rarely a husband or father of a family. . . . Being self-centered and bestial, Pulcinella had no scruples whatever, and because the moral suffering from his physical deformity reacted on his brain at the expense of his heart, he was exceedingly cruel. But Pulcinella grew mellower with age, and lapsed into a sort of second childhood which softened his cruelty into mere teasing and his sensuality into coarseness" (1966, 214–15). K. M. Lea describes how he is portrayed in many scenarios: "He is faithful, revengeful, sly, gullible, nervy, audacious, jealous, cowardly, bullying, sentimental, lazy, a scandalmonger, and full of malice in turn, and yet behind all these there is some common quality that we recognize as Pulcinella, just as we are aware of his nose and his accent when he disguises as a bride, a courier, a Spanish grandee, a thief, parrot, astrologer, Cupid, or a simple country-man" (1962, 1:100).

Maurice Sand describes two types inherent in the French Polichinelle adopted from the Italian *commedia*, "one, base and a fool, a true son of Maccus; the other, brazen, audacious, thieving, pugnacious, bohemian, of a more modern creation (quoted in Maindron 1900, 112, my translation). He perceived an expression of revolt in Polichinelle: "he is frightful, but he is terrific, rigorous, vindictive; it is neither God nor the devil who makes him tremble when he holds his big stick. With the aid of this instrument which he exerts on the shoulders of his master and on the necks of the public officers, he exercises a type of summary and individual justice, which avenges the foible of the iniquities of the official justice" (Maindron 1900, 108, my translation).

For Pierre Maindron, Polichinelle is "in turn burlesque, knavish, lustful, pugnacious, drunken, or cruel; he seems to be commissioned with materializing the vices inherent in poor humanity" (1900, 108, my translation). Maindron considers Polichinelle a type distinct from both Maccus and Pulcinella, having taken on the humor and temperament of a character specifically Gaulois. Maindron points to such qualities as a "frank and communicative laughter, which is truly the mask of a conscience in repose" and calls him "less perverse than Punch, for although he uses his stick freely, he does not kill." Maindron notes that the French Polichinelle appreciates women, is a good liver, a good drinker, an uninhibited user of salty language, completely lacks shame, and possesses an "unalterable gaiety" (1900, 113, my translation).

Polichinelle of the puppet theatre existed side by side with his *commedia* counterpart, performing in the theatrical milieu of the popular fairground. Whether he absorbed the *commedia* character or developed along parallel lines is an open question. Although restricted by a circumscribed physique and simplified gestural powers, his character perpetuated many of the above-mentioned character traits well after the demise of the *commedia* Polichinelle. Although the puppet character may lack the multi-dimensionality of the *commedia* character, he has always managed to combine a spurious amorality with limitless humor, a humor that is always on the edge, always unrestrained. The charm of a puppet Polichinelle lies in the simplicity with which he will blatantly violate acceptable behavior.

One of Polichinelle's earliest appearances as a puppet character can be traced to 1630, when he achieved great acclaim in the hands of Pierre Datelin, known as Brioché. Brioché was the founder of a dynasty of Parisian marionettists, rooted in the Paris fairgrounds (Sibbald 1936, 19). A children's folksong survives that may date from this period:

> *Pan! Pan! Qu'est-ce qu'est là?*
> *C'est Polichinelle qu'arrive.*
> *Il fait des pas, des poses et des grimaces*
> *Danse avec art*
> *Et fait le grand écart.* (Maindron 1900, 106)

(Knock! Knock! Who's there? It's Polichinelle who's come. He takes steps, strikes poses, and puts on airs, dances with style, and does the split.)

The most palpable difference between the original Pulcinella of the *commedia dell'arte* troupes and the Franco-Italian Polichinelle performed by the Comédie Italienne at the Hôtel Bourgogne in the latter half of the seventeenth century was a change of costume. This new mode was also reflected in the puppet figures, whereas the street performers at the fairgrounds tended to favor the earlier garb: a white, ample garment with a belt knotted at the waist, worn over loose, flowing pants; a wooden sword; and a black demi-mask from which projected a long, curved beak of a nose flanked by a large, pointy swirling moustache: "Over the years his costume became enriched: the doublet of beautiful material, terminating in points at the base of the stomach, evokes the male garment in fashion under Henry III, brother and successor to Charles IX. The two humps cause the sixteenth-century breastplate to bulge; in any event they confer a grotesque aspect to the character that was to contribute to his popularity" (David and Delrieu 1988, 25, my translation).

Brioché's Polichinelle is personified in a pamphlet in 1649, a political satire that takes the form of a letter from Polichinelle to Cardinal Jules Mazarin. Mazarin had presented his own religiously oriented puppet theatre, the Théatins, designed to serve a primarily pedagogic purpose. In a pamphlet, Brioché's Polichinelle pokes fun at Mazarin: "I can value myself without vanity, Messire Jules, since I have been always better welcomed than you by the people and better thought of, since I have so many times heard with my own ears: 'Let us go to see Polichinelle!' and nobody ever says 'Let us go to see Mazarin.' It is this that has caused me to be received like a noble bourgeois in Paris and you, on the other hand, you are chased like a louse from the church" (Maindron 1900, 115–16, my translation).

The period bracketed by the final quarter of the seventeenth century and the end of the eighteenth century can be considered a golden age for popular marionette theatre. It is a time when Polichinelle and his friend Arlequin are aligned with those struggling for the liberty of the French theatre. Stringent laws protected the privileges accorded the Opéra, the Comédie Française, and for a time, the Comédie Italienne, preserving these monopolies and suppressing the establishment of any new, competitive, independent theatrical venues. Several directors, whose theatres were disbanded due to the enforcement of such heavyhanded restrictions, turned to marionettes as an alternate expression, or as a way of maintaining their booths at the fairs, or to bring in income, or as a foundation for further, future attempts to establish their own new theatres.

Unlike actors, marionettes were allowed to speak freely, and even though, in their farces, they spoke the words of recognized authors, the content was considered innocuous or beneath contempt. In actuality, the marionettes often performed satires that were both social and literary and, at the least, provocative. Many, such as those presented by the marionettist Bienfait at the Foire Saint-Germain in 1732, were direct parodies of current productions at the Opéra and the Comédie (Sibbald 1936, 17–18).

Continued prolific marionette activity was found on the Boulevard du Temple, the Parisian promenade of popular entertainment that succeeded the Foire Saint-Germain and the Foire Saint-Laurent of the eighteenth century. Among the many marionettists operating there was Jean-Baptiste Nicolet, whose theatre received royal recognition, inspiring him to dub his marionettes "Les grands Danseurs du roi" (Sibbald 1936, 38). Later, after the Revolution, when the theatres were allowed to operate freely, Nicolet renamed his theatre "Théâtre de la Gaieté" and turned to using only live actors in his performances.

Another famous French theatre with roots in the popular marionette theatre of the Foire Saint-Germain and the Boulevard du Temple is the Ambigu Comique, founded by Nicholas-Médard Audinot. Famous for his *bamboches* or *comédiens du bois,* he used his marionettes to satirize his former fellow actors of the Opéra Comique with whom he had quarreled. He too later dispensed with marionettes altogether and presented child actors in his performances of "dialogued pantomime" (Sibbald 1936, 40).

Marionettes appear later in the Galléries du Palais Royale, successor to the Boulevard du Temple, in the hands of Gardeur and Delomel, who presented plays with songs and dances, vaudevilles, and parodies, among them *Figaro directeur de marionnettes.* By 1786, these marionettes too were entirely replaced by child actors. This occurrence is typical of the movement away from marionette theatre to popular living theatre that took place at the end of the eighteenth century (Sibbald 1936, 41).

The elaborate marionette theatres of Bienfait, Nicolet, Audinot, Gardeur, and Delomel utilized the *marionnette à fils,* the dancing stringed puppet, which was sometimes as large as three feet in height. Previous to, and coincidental with, these theatres were the simpler puppet performances utilizing the *marionnette à gaine,* the hand puppet, operating out of *castelets,* small, often collapsible, stage structures intended for one or two marionettists. The advent of a legitimate, affordable popular theatre certainly drew away audiences but did not efface the efforts of those marionettists who continued to perform and who moved further afield into the provinces.

The fairground outside of Lyons during the late eighteenth century is one of several places where Polichinelle could be found holding forth with an interlocutor-style puppet companion. It is there that Laurent Mourguet, who created his own puppet character, Guignol, would most likely have become acquainted with Polichinelle, who was to have a strong influence on his own creation. However, it was Guignol who gained ascendency in the nineteenth century. Polichinelle was relegated to second position, his plays presented less frequently, his role often becoming that of an introducer of the Guignol play. Although Guignol developed a character all his own that epitomized the personality of the struggling silk weaver, plucky, naive, and forever quipping no matter how desperate the situation, he stayed akin to Polichinelle in his roguery and odd high-pitched intonation.

The plots of the Guignol plays resemble the Polichinelle plays and also integrate the *commedia* tradition. They feature familiar casts of stock characters, deception, transformation, opposition to authority, combat between the sexes, sexual innuendo, compounded surprises, and high-spirited action. The verbal traditions of puns, repetitions, blunders, mis-understandings, and coexisting dialects are also the same. It should be stressed that through the character of Polichinelle, the quality of the *commedia dell'arte* permeated all of French puppet theatre.

Although Polichinelle never disappeared altogether, he certainly maintained a lower profile in France during the latter half of the nineteenth century. Nevertheless, he seems to have successfully resisted the sentimentality of nineteenth-century French theatre and retained his physical grotesqueness and truculent voice even in the subsidiary roles of interlocutor or master of ceremonies.

Traditional puppetry has persisted in France into the twentieth century, and although it is still valued as an art form by many and is unquestionably a part of the everyday life of the very young, its presence has been sporadic. I would like to take a look at one instance where traditional puppetry continues to flourish, and in so doing, chronicle a contemporary emergence of Polichinelle.

Philippe Casidanus is one of the people who is helping to keep traditional French puppet theatre alive. He is the resident puppeteer in the Parc Georges Brassens, on the southern edge of Paris. Americans who have watched the televised language course "French in Action" on PBS have seen his Guignol and Polichinelle at the close of every episode.

Casidanus is a tall, lanky man with unruly blond hair, an engaging smile, and a semi-permanent stoop from bending down behind his puppet stage. He came to traditional marionette theatre by an unusual route. Aside from childhood exposure to Guignol in the park, he first encountered puppet theatre while part of the student movement in 1968. His training as an actor led him to take part in a political play, which he describes as an audiovisual montage that made use of short marionette scenes to create a sort of passion play about General Franco after he had banned a play by Armand Gatti. Casidanus described the odd sensation of playing to an audience of 2,000 eagerly trying to catch a glimpse of the little marionettes and to hear every sound emanating from the tiny theatre. He continued to work in nontraditional puppet theatre with both informal and established groups, among them the Yves Vedrenne company.

In 1974, Casidanus founded the "Théâtre de la Trille aux loups" and performed in universities and at festivals. In 1978, he worked with Jose Luis Gonsales and put on the play *Vie et mort de Lazarillo des Tormes,* an adaptation of the sixteenth-century Spanish picaresque tale. His move into traditional marionette theatre took place in 1980, when he was offered the succession of the Castelet du Vrai Guignolet of the Champs-Elysées by Auguste Guentfleur, who had been marionettist there for fifty years and was the last of a dynasty of marionettists performing there since 1818. He continued to direct the theatre at the Champs-Elysées while moving to the Parc Georges Brassens in 1988. He initially performed Guignol and then branched out to perform Polichinelle in 1989. He now performs Polichinelle exclusively.

Casidanus operates out of an unheated building not far from the carousel and the playground within a large, beautiful Parisian park. The building is a simple cement structure approximately twenty by forty feet, with attractive closed-in windows along the sides, surrounded by hedges. His puppet stage, approximately five feet wide, three feet deep and four feet high, takes up the front of the room. Approximately twenty rows of long, narrow benches face the stage.

His is a one-person operation. He rings the handbell before performances, collects admission (about two dollars), and makes sure that the smaller spectators get the front benches; then he handles the movement of the puppets, the dialogue, the lighting, and the sound effects during the performance. He also creates the texts, many of the properties, and some of the backdrops, and makes repairs on his own puppets when needed.

Casidanus's performance, which lasts approximately forty-five minutes, is subtly and artistically conceived and executed and is clearly appreciated by both adults and children. He interjects humorous asides that differ from performance to performance but do not seem to disturb the authentic flavor of his plays. His voice and diction are superb. His choice of material is perfectly suited to his audience, though slightly above the level of its youngest members. He strikes an immediate rapport by directly questioning his audience and persistently awaiting a response that is always forthcoming.

In his performance of *Le tonneau magique,* Casidanus relied heavily on a puppet character, Martin, who was unfamiliar to me as a character in the Polichinelle repertoire. He later revealed that he had invented Martin because his particular Polichinelle, an authentic antique puppet, is too heavy for him to manipulate continuously for an entire performance. Casidanus showed me the inner workings of his *castelet*, where he hangs the waiting puppets during the performance, and how he creates some of his special effects. He also demonstrated his daily ritual of warming-up hand positions, which he described as a sort of *ta'i chi* for the marionettist. In Casidanus's words, "My artistic goal is to continue the tradition, but with a contemporary sensibility enriched by historic texts, and to add new characters. The texts are improvisations on skeleton texts of the Italian *commedia dell'arte*."

His views on a possible division between traditional and contemporary puppet theatre are optimistic, and perhaps charitable: "The division between traditional and modern marionettists is a false problem. I think that each one influences the other, the modern are influenced by the origins, and the traditional are not insensible to new techniques, for example, tape recording, microphone, amplification, tricks of lighting. I think that the new modern marionette troupes also have helped the public to develop a desire to get to know the traditional marionettes. For example, more and more marionette festivals are beginning to invite traditional marionettists to come present their work" (Letter to author, January 21, 1991, my translation).

I find Casidanus's aesthetic unusual and refreshing. In his own work, he has achieved a graceful blend of traditional and contemporary elements that is by no means the norm. In spite of the introduction of contemporary elements, the work of Casidanus retains many aspects of the *commedia* tradition. In terms of the scenario, the plot often revolves around having Polichinelle trying to accomplish some mission that is simply a pretext for a string of episodes that make up the dramatic action. Polichinelle may be ostensibly trying to deliver a coffer of jewels, but in the course of that effort he may become lost in a forest, lose the coffer, find the coffer, encounter a bandit, fight with a *gendarme*, fight with a crocodile, be helped by a genie or sorcerer, fight the devil, or be transformed into the devil himself by the sorcerer. In the end, he triumphs; the coffer is recovered and restored. He usually travels with a partner—a servant, a friend, or even his son—whom he takes delight in tricking in some way or involving in some of his pranks.

The dialogue moves quickly, replete with puns, blundering misunderstandings, repetitions, and the exaggerated accents of the *gendarme* or brigand. Polichinelle's own speech pattern is a survival of the Neopolitan Pulcinella. Although Casidanus does not place a metallic whistle in his mouth, the traditional means of creating the raucous, chicken-like voice of Polichinelle (Gascar 1980, 41), he gives the voice a consistently distinctive, high-pitched, piercing tone and odd rhythmic delivery.

Casidanus's Polichinelle is somewhat cryptic in character. He often speaks in monosyllables, as if keeping some secret plan close to himself, and then suddenly erupts in a fountain of verbosity. He is mischievous and malevolent. He likes to confuse his compatriots and crow over their discomfiture while he will unhesitatingly beat up an adversary. He is nasty, but less blatantly so than his forebear. Casidanus describes his Polichinelle as "a mean mouth, an impulsive, the gossip who doesn't mince words, the arrogant one who disturbs the established order" (Letter to author, March 5, 1992, my translation). Casidanus's Polichinelle puppet figure visually delineates the earlier prototypical comic ideal in its widely drawn, sensual, leering lips, protruding beak nose, bright, laughing eyes, enormous hump, and big, self-indulgent belly. As a puppet it is even more exaggerated.

In his current exploit, Polichinelle leaves for Naples, accompanied by his faithful friend Pierrot, to come to the aid of Pulcinella, whose theatre is in danger of destruction by Monsieur Mangetout, who plans to construct a sausage factory in its place. Polichinelle discovers his lineage in Pulcinella. The two embrace and display their virtuosity in dances and pirouettes. In a sort of initiation ordeal, Polichinelle's patience is tested by misadventures that afford him the opportunity to display his philosophy of insolence. With the cooperation of an evil genie he is able to redress the score by trapping the bad capitalist in a barrel full of gold coins.

This contemporary version of the Polichinelle puppet theatre is easily associated with the *commedia dell'arte* through its treatment of an episodic scenario, stock characters, deception, transformation, opposition to authority, high-spirited action, verbal patterns, and characterization. Its informal mode of performance and resulting reception, characterized by uproarious audience participation, calls to mind similar spectacles at the seventeenth-century fairgrounds.

So far we have focused on the similarities between *commedia* and puppet theatre, yet the differences also provide insight on how the puppet medium can serve to further the spirit of *commedia*. The use of the mask in *commedia* effected the distance needed to convey an aura of unreality to otherwise commonplace situations and made possible the acceptance of simplified and exaggerated personality traits that would have been unacceptable in a conventional theatrical setting. The portrayals of numerous artists from Callot to Tiepolo show us that the *commedia* actor was extremely physical and made larger-than-life gestures in an effort to represent exaggerated character types; the simplified rude gestures of the puppet create a similar exaggerated effect. In puppetry, the puppet, acting as an animated object, can serve the same function as a mask. A flesh-and-blood actor would elicit a certain amount of compassion from us if he or she were afflicted by a gross physical disability such as a hump. But we can comfortably laugh at a puppet who sustains beatings and humiliations, knowing that it is only made of wood. The informal setting of the puppet theatre furthers an ambience in which the puppeteer is expected to play off audience response and vary the rhythm of delivery accordingly. The very nature of such a performance space encourages a free-flowing improvisatory style that is integral to the *commedia* tradition. For all these reasons, Polichinelle as puppet can be seen to be a legitimate heir to his *commedia* forebear, and the puppet stage an imaginative context in which the legacy of *commedia dell'arte* may be expressed and developed.

Works Cited

Caputi, Anthony. *Buffo*. Detroit: Wayne State University Press, 1978.

D'Aponte, Mimi. "*La Canzone di Zeza*." *Italian Quarterly* 28:107 (Winter 1987): 71–104.

David, Martine, and Anne-Marie Delrieu. *Refrains d'enfance*. Paris: Herscher, 1988.

Duchartre, Pierre Louis. *The Italian Comedy*. Translated by Randolph T. Weaver. 1929. Reprint. New York: Dover Publications, 1966.

Gascar, Pierre. *Le Boulevard du Crime*. Paris: Hachette/Massin, 1980.

Lea, K. M. *Italian Popular Comedy*. 2 vols. 1934. Reprint. New York: Russell and Russell, 1962.

Maindron, Ernest. *Marionnettes et Guignols*. Paris: F. Juven, 1900.

Nicoll, Allardyce. *Masks, Mimes and Miracles*. New York: Cooper Square Publishers, 1963.

Sibbald, Reginald S. *Marionettes in the North of France*. Lancaster, PA: University of Pennsylvania Press, 1936.

Smith, Winifred. *The Commedia dell'Arte*. New York: Columbia University Press, 1912.

Controversy, Cops, and *Commedia*

Staging the Throwaway Farce of Fo's
Accidental Death of an Anarchist

James Fisher

Don't call my play a comedy. There is a misunderstanding of the word. I call it farce. In current language, farce is understood as vulgar, trivial, facile, very simple. In truth, this is a cliché of official culture. What they call comedy today has lost the rebellious strain of ancient times. What is provocative and rebellious is farce. The establishment goes for comedy, the people for farce.

(Fo 1984)

The revival of *commedia dell'arte* in twentieth-century theatres is a plot with many twists. For some modern artists, *commedia* has supplied performance techniques emphasizing the role of masks, improvisation, and the actor's centrality. For others, *commedia* has meant liberation from the pervasiveness of the naturalistic stage and the dominance of the playwright. For still others, *commedia* represents a return to the world of the anarchic clown and the atmosphere of the street carnival. And, for a few, *commedia* has been a vehicle for political empowerment.

One thing seems certain: that virtually any approach to reproducing the effect of *commedia* in a modern performance implies a free, spirited, and open exchange not only between the actors and the audience, but also between the actors and their play. The basic nature of *commedia* rests on its immediacy and its assault of power structures, small and large. Since the 1960s, Italy's Dario Fo (b. 1926) as a playwright, actor, and director has looked to the various aspects of modern *commedia* in his politically controversial plays. He has brought together the work of the actor and the author to address both the actor's and the audience's own immediate issues in performances that invite a significant exchange of ideas between the audience and the play.

Even before he was aware of the traditions of *commedia,* Fo explored performance techniques like those found in *commedia,* inspired in equal parts by the plays and performances of his countrymen Luigi Pirandello, Ettore Petrolini, and Eduardo de Filippo. Fo became a popular success as a comic actor in the 1950s before he realized that "in order to create a discipline, you have to have an ideology. In my opinion it is extremely dangerous to practice in the theatrical arts without knowing what *end* this practice is supposed to serve" (Fo and Rame 1983, back cover). Fo's end has since been clearly in sight: Marxism as an ideology with a focus on examining the social, economic, moral, and political plights of the middle and lower classes.

Fo's stage persona is the anarchic clown; he came to the theatre, he notes, not "to play Hamlet, but with the aspiration to be the red-nosed comic, the clown" (Fo 1991, 84). His admiration of clowns and fools is founded in the performance traditions of *commedia,* as well as in the *giullari,* the grotesque medieval street entertainers whom he refers to as "the rag-and-bone men who wore the masks" (Fo 1991, 7). Written hurriedly and often depending on improvisation, Fo's "throwaway" plays are similar to newspaper articles or debates. A play is temporary in Fo's view; it must remain forever open to change and continuing reaction to topical events. His most representative works are grotesque farcical documentaries that satirize governmental and industrial corruption, and the resultant problems of survival for the middle and lower classes. Thus, it is perhaps not surprising that Fo views the clown as a blasphemous voice of the people, an alter ego for the masses. Most of his plays call for radical social change and nonviolent revolution, featuring a profaneness and outrageousness typical, in Fo's mind, of "the liberating role" (Fo 1991, 47) of improvising *commedia* actors. Fo's work mixes seriousness of purpose with *commedia*-inspired farce and can be best understood as an explosive, creative reaction to the harsh realities of life.

Fo has drawn inspiration from circus, puppetry, carnivals, music halls, *teatro del grottesco,* Punch and Judy, and, most obviously, *commedia.* He does not accept *commedia* as generic and pure, but as a form in which there are distinctly variant styles. He acknowledges that there is "a *part* of the *commedia dell'arte*" which he has absorbed and used for his radical political plays, but stresses that many of the original *commedia* troupes, such as the Gelosi, were "generally conservative, and often downright reactionary in content" because of the patronage these troupes accepted from the Italian nobility. He suggests that the great *commedia* troupes were "a bit like those football teams nowadays that are owned by big industrialists" (Fo and Rame 1983, 8).

By the mid-1950s, having once mastered the techniques of the *commedia*-inspired actor and mime, Fo set out to learn the necessary skills of playwriting, seeking models in the great comic plays of Plautus, Shakespeare, and Molière, as well as Pirandello and de Filippo, but not with the goal of creating a polished work of dramatic literature. In fact, Fo believes that such works are antithetical to his kind of drama: "Theatre has nothing to do with literature, even when, by fair means or foul, people go out of their way to force it into line. . . . However paradoxical it may seem, a genuine work of theatre should not at all appear a pleasure when read: its worth should only become apparent on the stage" (Fo 1991, 183). Fo's plays, like sporting events, are not static or permanently fixed. Even his best-known, most-produced works have undergone continual revisions to keep them as fresh as today's headlines. Fo believes that the freelance *commedia* performers, who had a significant and immediate influence on the life of the general populace, are worthy of emulation. They were "professionals, who didn't frequent the courts and nobility, but worked in taverns, worked in town squares, worked in far lowlier circumstances" (Fo 1991, 183). To recreate *commedia,* Fo insists that "you have to decide which political line, which cultural direction you are going to take as the basis for your work" (Fo 1991, 183). His clearly articulated mission is to "advance certain democratic appeals, to form public opinion, to stimulate, to create moments of dialectical conflict" (Carlson 1984, 477). As Fo emphasizes, "There is a community dimension in performing theatre, and the characters are a pretext to make the people 'speak'" (Fo 1985, 135). For Fo, and all such artists, "It goes without saying that all theatre, and all art, is political" (Fo 1985, 131). He believes that the connection between politics and improvisation is total: "The choice of an improvisational form of theatre is already a political one—because improvisational theatre is never finished, never a closed case, always open-ended" (D'Aponte 1989, 537). Fo depends on satire to make his social and political statements, believing that "nothing gets down as deeply into the mind and intelligence as satire. . . . The end of satire is the first alarm bell signalling the end of real democracy" (Fo 1979, 15).

Among Fo's most political plays derived from *commedia* tradition is *Accidental Death of an Anarchist,* a "grotesque farce about a tragic farce" (Fo 1984, 11), which opened at the Capannone, a former factory converted into a theatre in Milan's Via Colletta on December 10, 1970, under Fo's direction and featuring him in the leading role.[1] Virtually a

---

[1]*Accidental Death of an Anarchist* was first produced in the United States in January 1983 at the Mark Taper Forum in Los Angeles in an adaptation by John Lahr. The next attempt came in February 1984 at the Arena Theatre, Washington, D.C., followed by a short run at

"living newspaper" with a jazz improvisation style, this Italian agit-prop work presents the events surrounding the actual 1969 bombing of the Agricultural Bank in Milan. Following the incident, an anarchist named Giovanni Pinelli was arrested. Shortly thereafter, when Pinelli was killed in a fall from a fourth-floor window in police headquarters, the police and local officials claimed that the anarchist had committed suicide. It is at this point that Fo begins his Ortonesque lunacy of counter information, exposing the lies and cover-ups perpetrated by the police who, as it turns out, pushed the anarchist from the window to his death. As Fo describes it, the plot involves a Maniac "who gets inside a police station and puts the police on trial, reversing the usual process" (Fo 1985, 133). Fo's alter-ego, the Maniac, becomes a one-man carnival employing a variety of disguises and subterfuges in an ultimately successful attempt to expose the distortions and lies of the "official" version of the "suicide" told by the police. In fact, the actual trial of the police was going on when Fo mounted the original production, and each performance was altered to bring in the latest news from the trial. Fo also managed to find lawyers, court officials, and reporters who would feed him copies of unpublished evidence and documents related to the case.

In staging *Accidental Death of an Anarchist* in November 1991 at Wabash College (Crawfordsville, Indiana), I emphasized Fo's use of *commedia*-inspired elements in order to expose tragic events, and although the audience became aware that they were watching an outrageous farce, they were never permitted to forget the play's disturbing base in reality. The play must at once function on at least three different temporal levels: the era in which Fo wrote the play (1970), the time period in which Fo's play was adapted by the translator,[2] and the present. The original play, of course, contributes the story of Pinelli's death at the hands of the police, the diverse adaptations bring in a variety of updated references, and the production must make the most topical and localized references. The Wabash production included comments on George Bush and Dan Quayle, apartheid, the AIDS epidemic, the Clarence Thomas

---

the Belasco Theatre, New York, opening November 15, 1984 (this version was adapted by Richard Nelson and directed by Douglas C. Wager). Perhaps the most successful American production was presented at the Eureka Theater, San Francisco, in November 1984, in an adaptation by Joan Holden, directed by Anthony Taccone.

[2]There are at least half a dozen English translations available. The script for the Wabash production was pieced together out of two versions of the play, the 1983 London version and the 1984 Broadway version, because while the London version offered the most effective ending and the sharpest satire, the Broadway version offered references to American issues and the most colloquial speech.

hearings, the Savings and Loan scandal, and the beating of Rodney King by the Los Angeles police, an especially potent topical reference since it related directly to Fo's dominant theme.

The Wabash production emphasized these three temporal levels in several ways; most obviously, it pushed away from any naturalistic tendencies. The single set, which served as two different offices in the Milan police station, was constructed on platforms with the supports below and stage braces behind the set exposed. Lighting instruments were close to the acting area and clearly visible to the audience. In addition, at the stage right side, a "dressing room" with costumes, a makeup table, mirrors, dress dummies, etc., was added. Here, the Maniac could leave the police station scene to experiment with his various disguises while also talking directly to the audience, allowing for updated political and local references not part of either Fo's original play or any of the subsequent translations/adaptations. This approach is invited by the text itself, which includes comic references to Fo, as when one of the policemen, Inspector Bertozzo, ironically announces to the audience that "the author of this sick little play, Dario Fo, has the traditional, irrational hatred of the police common to all narrow-minded left-wingers and so I shall, no doubt, be the unwilling butt of endless anti-authoritarian jibes" (Fo 1987, 2).

Along with the "dressing room," on the stage right side of the acting area there was an exposed "backstage area" with the stage manager and some lighting and sound equipment visible, along with a waiting area for the actors who were not actually onstage. This area also included a piano, which was used at the end of Act One and the beginning of Act Two when the cast invites the audience to join them in singing the *Internationale*. One of the actors leaps offstage to play the piano while the other actors, as well as the stage manager, gather around the piano to sing, and, finally, to march out of the theatre through the audience. The second act begins with the *Internationale,* as the actors march back into the theatre singing and return to the same moment that ended the first act.

As in traditional *commedia,* the interplay between actor and audience is central to the effectiveness of this play. To accentuate that interplay, and to make the comic dislocation of the play clearer, the actors, in costume and makeup, took tickets and handed out programs at the theatre door, mingling with the audience before the play began and during intermission. The actors playing the oppressive policemen comically harassed audience members, questioning "suspicious" looking patrons or "frisking" others. All of this mingling seemed useful in terms of breaking down the fourth wall and allowing for an informal, relaxed environment. As well, whenever the Maniac broke out of a scene, he either moved into the dressing-room area or out into the audience, breaking through the fourth wall and developing a closer relationship with the audience throughout the play. Actors waiting in the visible offstage area led audience reactions to the action and, at two points, chases involved the actors leaving the stage and running through the audience.

One problem in doing a play like this for an American audience is that it seems we are less accustomed to Fo's politicized notion of the clown than we are to the bland, empty clowning typical of modern circuses. It seemed important to help the audience understand Fo's brand of clowns, and, inspired by Fo's interest in masks and his emphasis on the value of employing the most popular theatrical genres to advance his political views, the production looked to silent film comedy to find images for the individual characters. Makeup in silent film comedies was boldly overdone and only a step away from an actual mask. Under stark lighting this sort of makeup takes on a grotesque, almost eerie quality. The Maniac became the Chaplinesque figure, of course, and the actors playing the policemen drew their inspirations from a range of silent screen villains and the Keystone Kops. However, despite these images, emphasis was placed on maintaining both a sense of the actor himself and the brutality inherent in Fo's vision of these characters. The visibility of the actor within the character was accentuated by those points when one of them broke out of character and the actors would call each other by their real names. Fo's brutality was maintained in moments when the comic slapstick escalated to startlingly real violence. At carefully selected moments, the hilarity stopped abruptly and a brief but savage roughness emerged.

The makeup seemed to liberate the actors to a great degree, since they felt both the security that wearing masks can provide and a more vivid sense of their characters and the style of acting required. In his writings on the mask, Fo has discussed the "third eye" of the mask, a red stamp that was, according to Fo, historically present on the masks of the *zanni,* as well as on some oriental masks. For Fo this third eye "serves to indicate the diabolic character of the mask" (Fo 1991, 34) and liberates that aspect of the actor who wears it. To a significant degree, the actors found their "third eye" through diabolic makeup inspired by silent film comedy.

The character of the Maniac is the most problematic in the play, since Fo created the role for himself. Like any role tailor-made to an actor's talents, it may not be a comfortable fit for others. The role is both intensely physical *and* intensely verbal, and Fo's notion of the "third eye" is essential in the case of this character. There is much slapstick throughout, particularly as the Maniac rapidly switches disguises and literally dances around the befuddled policemen. One absurd disguise involves a wooden leg and a wooden hand as the Maniac escalates his trickery to the totally outrageous. The Maniac is most adept in the manipulation of language, as he must use it to best the policemen's manipulation of the truth. He must seem a madman to the police, as well as to the audience at the start of the play, but ultimately the audience must come to see that the madman makes sense while the world he battles proves to be mad. As with the roles in the plays of Brecht, in the acting of this part (and most of Fo's characters) the actor must represent the character. To accomplish this representation, the actor must act in the third person, as "a 'call boy' who represents the character to the audience, props it up or humiliates it, reports it or condemns it, hates it or loves it, as the case requires" (Fo 1991, 136). The Maniac talks directly to the audience in lengthy political diatribes specifically on the issue of police corruption in the play and also on a kaleidoscopic variety of political and social scandals and injustices. At one point near the end of the play, the Maniac leaps from the stage and begins to rattle off a chronicle of these injustices only to be interrupted by one of the other characters who shouts, "Wait a minute! This is not Dario Fo. This is an unheard of distortion of the author's meaning!" "Tough shit," replies the Maniac, "I've got something to say. He'll get his royalties. Who's moaning?" (Fo 1987, 68).

The characters of the four policemen (the Officer, the Inspector, the Captain, and the Superintendent) are problematic in different ways, although these actors too must represent their characters. All of them are involved in the murder of the anarchist and the subsequent cover-up, but it seemed necessary in production to build a hierarchy of power within this gang of four, with the Officer at the bottom and the Superintendent at the top. As implications of their individual crimes are revealed, each attempts to pass the responsibility on to another, with, of course, the Officer at the bottom getting most of it dumped on him.

The only remaining character is a reporter, Maria Feletti. Since Wabash is an all-male college, and since the role did not seem to require a particular gender, Maria Feletti became Mario Feletti. This character enters the play late, inspiring another change of disguise for the Maniac, and serving to introduce deeper levels of corruption to the point of implicating the entire society. Feletti is also a voice of moderation, arguing with the police over their outrageous lies and the Maniac over his extremist position. In the ending we presented at Wabash, based on the London production, two final scenes were shown. Feletti became essential in demonstrating the inherent failure of a moderate approach; only a complete and continual revolution offers any true hope.

What the play and its variant productions finally suggest is that Fo's clown and those of the original *commedia dell'arte* deal with a similar problem, "be it hunger for food, for sex, or even for dignity, for identity, for power. The problem they invariable pose is—who's in command, who's the boss?" (Fo 1991, 172)

Works Cited

Carlson, Marvin. *Theories of the Theatre*. Ithaca and London: Cornell University Press, 1984.

D'Aponte, Mimi. "From Italian Roots to American Relevance: The Remarkable Theatre of Dario Fo." *Modern Drama* 32:4 (December 1989): 532–44.

Fo, Dario. *Pum, pum! Chi è? La polizia!* Verona: Bertani, 1984.

———. "Dialogue with an Audience." *Theatre Quarterly* 9:35 (Autumn 1979): 11–16.

———. Program Note for the Arena Theatre (Washington, D.C.) production of *Accidental Death of an Anarchist*. 1984.

———. "Some Aspects of Popular Theatre." Translated by Tony Mitchell. *New Theatre Quarterly* 1:2 (May 1985): 131–37.

———. *Accidental Death of an Anarchist*. Adapted by Gavin Richards from a translation by Gillian Hanna. London: Methuen, 1987.

———. *Tricks of the Trade*. Translated by Joe Farrell. Edited and with notes by Stuart Hood. New York: Routledge/Theatre Arts, 1991.

Fo, Dario, and Franca Rame. *Theatre Workshops at Riverside Studios, London, April 28th, May 5th, 12th, 13th, & 19th, 1983*. London: Red Notes, 1983.

Commedia in the Classroom

Commedia dell'Arte Performance,
Shakespearean Pedagogy,
and Popular Culture

Georgeann Murphy

*W*RITING RECENTLY in the *Atlantic Monthly* about students who not only read less, but understand less of what they read, Daniel Singal addresses with frightening clarity what he calls "the context of ignorance" (1991). Singal attributes the difficulty many American college students have assimilating new knowledge to their lack of a larger intellectual context for that knowledge: details slip quickly away when you can't relate them to something you already know. Singal's point recalled to me my maiden shock as a high school freshman reading Shakespeare for the first time: plots seemed overwhelmingly complex and characters incomprehensibly bizarre. I was at the time more flummoxed than fascinated. Now, as a teacher of Shakespeare, I often begin courses by acknowledging some of the reasons why reading him is so difficult. Great gulfs separate us from both the culture and the language of late sixteenth-, early seventeenth-century London. Shifts of vowel values, meaning, and nuance are not the only difficulties in understanding Shakespeare's language, for frequently that language is poetic, the most compressed—sometimes even metaphysical—form of expression. Most discomfitingly of all, the "text" of a Shakespearean play is not on the page but on the stage. Performance is the radical context of Shakespearean drama, but most college students have no experience envisioning a script as action and know little of performance conventions.

Even theatre students with, perhaps, more performance experience than most undergraduates need practice developing their theatrical imaginations. To overcome this particular barrier to understanding, teachers try many tricks: taking classes to performances or (the more likely scenario) showing videotapes; stressing in class not only the *mythos, ethos, dianoia,* and *lexis* of a scene, but also the *melos* and the *opsis;* getting students to act scenes out in class—often with singularly disappointing results. While all these efforts can be helpful in varying degrees, I have found none so effective as placing Shakespeare within the context of a tradition of popular performance, which even the most unread students will be surprised to discover they know rather a lot about. What I propose here is a teaching strategy for making that connection. Bringing *commedia* into the classroom can help students apply what they already know to what seems at first formidable about Shakespeare.

Not that most students will recognize the term *commedia dell'arte.* They most likely won't know of Atellan farce or Plautus and Terence either. But the gestalt of situation and character apparent in these, in Shakespeare, and in *commedia* they do know very well. How? From long-running and re-running television sitcoms—shows like *All in the Family, M*A*S*H,* and *Cheers*—episodes of which students often know by heart. Placing Shakespeare in the context of a popular performance tradition stretching from the earliest beginnings of Western drama through *commedia dell'arte* right on to contemporary syndicated megahits on television can help students recognize their own culture as part of a continuing, conservative comic tradition. *Commedia* performances preserved comic patterns which students will find familiar and can use to interpret the unfamiliar.

These patterns do not, in fact, belong exclusively to comedy: there are Pantalones in *Hamlet* and *Othello*[1] as well as in *The Taming of the Shrew* and *A Midsummer Night's Dream.* Finding the *commedia* types in whatever Shakespearean play is under discussion can be a profitable heuristic game that prompts students to detect a figure in the carpet, a repeating pattern of characteristics and behavior that not only defines a type, but also makes more apparent the significance of deviating from the type. Many critics have identified *commedia* characters in Shakespeare, and standard studies like those of Lea and Herrick have painstakingly traced connections between Shakespeare, his contemporaries, and Italian comedy.[2] But before engaging in a classroom Pantalone-hunt, it is important to introduce students to Shakespeare's saturation in the larger current of influence flowing from the Italian to the English Renaissance: beginning with Sir Thomas Hoby's 1561 translation of Castiglione's

---

[1]For the relationship of *Othello* to *commedia* traditions, see Teague 1986 and Zancha 1969.

[2]See, for example, Lea [1934] 1962, vol. 2, and Herrick 1960.

The Courtier, one can document the arrival of a new age in England with Italian translations (McWilliam 1974, 8). The Shakespearean canon itself provides remarkable evidence of Italian influence: of Shakespeare's thirty-eight plays, twenty-two have obvious Italian connections—Italian or classical Latin sources and/or Italianate settings. Probably Shakespeare relied on translations and adaptations of his Italian sources: no one has yet proven his knowledge of the language (in fact, the Spanish knight in *Pericles* speaks Italian, indicating either Shakespeare's notorious indifference to editing or some linguistic confusion). It also seems unlikely that a playwright capable of real geographical howlers had any firsthand knowledge of the lay of Italian land—in *The Taming of the Shrew,* people come ashore in land-locked Padua (1.1.42), and a rich merchant of that city boasts he is the owner of "an argosy / That now is lying in Marseilles' road" (2.1.372). But the connection between Shakespeare and Italian influence does not depend on firsthand knowledge, any more than a taste for *fettuccine all'Alfredo* and Milanese-inspired fashion implies a knowledge of Italy or Italian.

Probably there will be someone in your class with a penchant for pasta and/or Italian design who can help make the point that popular culture is currently a global matter. Allowing for longer transmission time—fads traveled more slowly in the sixteenth and seventeenth centuries because news and people did—not much has changed, and Shakespeare certainly knew of *commedia* players. It is possible that he had immediate contact with them: there are records of Italian comedians in England as early as 1546 (Lea [1934] 1962, 2:352), eighteen years before Shakespeare's birth. The famous early company, the Gelosi, performed from 1568 to 1604, a period incorporating the first half of Shakespeare's theatrical career; it isn't a stretch to imagine an ambitious young playwright hearing about—and using—*commedia* material. Furthermore, Shakespeare's plays actually refer to improvising comedians, magnificoes, pantaloons, pedants, and zanies.[3] Imitation was, after all, an aesthetic principle in the English Renaissance, the rule rather than the exception. In fact, the *New York Times* reports in a recent "Arts & Leisure" cover story (Horowitz 1992) that plagiarizing good stories and characters remains a legally troublesome fact in our own entertainment industry. Again, not much has changed.

---

[3]For example, *1 Henry IV* (2.4.276) and *Antony and Cleopatra* (5.2.216) refer to improvised comedy; *The Merchant of Venice* (3.2.280) and *Othello* (1.2.12) refer to the Magnifico; *The Taming of the Shrew* (3.1.36) and *As You Like It* (2.7.157) refer to the Pantaloon; *Love's Labours Lost* (5.2.539), *The Taming of the Shrew* (4.2.64), and *Twelfth Night* (1.5.86) refer to the Zany. See Mellamphy 1980, 150.

Shakespeare, a more savvy, if not more ethical businessman than some Hollywood producers, was additionally a writer of real genius. He appropriated *commedia* types and situations and "morphed" them to suit his own purposes, combining and superimposing traits to create something new with a skill the technical wizards behind the *Terminator* films and Michael Jackson videos would envy. Having established that, one must next point out to students that *commedia* and Shakespeare share an inherited tradition dating at least as far back as the stock situations and types of Greek New Comedy, especially as rendered by the Roman comic writers Plautus (c. 254–184 B.C.). and Terence (c. 186–159 B.C.). Many attempts have been made to trace *commedia dell'arte's* origins from these classical sources through the rustic regional dialect farces prevalent in Italy during the Middle Ages all the way to the sixteenth century. Shakespeare's education at the King's New School in Stratford inspires just as much critical speculation about the influence of that learning on his plays. Almost certainly his instruction included the imitation of plays by both Plautus and Terence, an exercise in dramatic structure as well as Latin, which would have introduced him to the stock characters and situations of Roman comedy. In the classroom it is easy to make the point that popular Roman comedy informs both the *commedia dell'arte* play and the Shakespearean script. Students who know something about classical comedy or *commedia* will recognize in Shakespeare classical/ *commedia* types. But such recognition need not belong only to the initiated. A quick précis of the major characters will allow everyone to play the game.

They are everywhere: the servants/*zanni*/Arlecchinos of the stupid, ever-hungry variety—like Gobbo of *The Merchant of Venice,* the Dromios of *The Comedy of Errors,* Lance and Speed in *Two Gentlemen of Verona,* Stephano and Trinculo of *The Tempest;* the clever servants/*zanni*/ Brighellas like Tranio in *The Taming of the Shrew* and Puck of *A Midsummer Night's Dream;* the heavy fathers/Pantalones like Brabantio in *Othello,* Shylock in *The Merchant of Venice,* and Polonius in *Hamlet;* the pedants/ Dottores like Holofernes in *Love's Labours Lost* or, again, Polonius with his ragman's roll of generic categories; the braggart soldiers/Capitanos like Don Armado in *Love's Labours Lost,* Parolles of *All's Well That Ends Well,* or Falstaff, a brilliant elaboration of a type; the lovers/Innamorati of all the plays; and the *caratteri,* dialect characters of the histories like Fluellen, Jamy, and MacMorris. Additionally, the typical *commedia* plot, with its reliance on cuckolding; the misunderstandings and confusions of lovers; strange adventures and intrigues like shipwrecks, kidnappings, and magic spells; indomitable passions, disguises (including women dressed as men and twins mistaken for each other), night scenes, repetitions, and frank vulgarity,[4] easily compares with plot elements in practically all Shakespeare's comedies and romances. The Reduced Shakespeare Company, a currently touring troupe, has in fact built a career of distilling all these elements into one generic Shakespearean comedy. Students have fun doing the same, and because one can't burlesque a form without first understanding it, that too is a useful classroom exercise.

Reading or seeing some *commedia* along with their Shakespeare makes Shakespeare's dramatic conventions more evident to students. I have found my students also enjoy hearing about performance practices and how *commedia* troupes and Shakespeare's had more in common than plots and characters. Shakespeare wrote, after all, for a relatively small company of actors, each with a specialty well known to him (Burbage did not play Kempe's roles, nor Kempe Burbage's). Shakespeare's plays privilege character in the same way *commedia* plays do. Both *commedia* companies and Shakespeare's survived through a combination of patronage and public support. *Commedia* plays, like Shakespeare's, make the most of verbal wit as well as buffoonery. Both rely on song and dance. The more students read Shakespeare, the more they come to recognize his own characteristic *lazzi* and *concetti*, comic turns and conceits. Neither Shakespeare nor most *commedia* performers were much interested in preserving their scripts on the printed page, a fact infinitely delightful to students laboring to deconstruct a text. The problem of finding an authoritative text of Shakespearean and *commedia* plays can intrigue students and is fundamental to the most significant correspondence between Shakespeare and the *commedia:* both are examples of popular performance art.

This last connection will allow you to make the final pedagogical leap to our own popular culture and the survival of *commedia* types in TV situation comedies. As this point, the professor truly empowers the students, who almost certainly know more about TV than their teacher. The challenge is to spot the Pantalones, Arlecchinos, Brighellas, Dottores, and Capitanos still populating American television. The most likely common ground will be long-running, now syndicated shows like *M*A*S*H, All in the Family,* or *SOAP.* From such fertile fields students will quickly unearth Archie Bunker/Pantalone, a heavy father who is avaricious, slanderous, and quarrelsome; Frank Burns/Capitano, a lustful, braggart coward; Radar O'Reilly/Brighella, a servant so clever that he is prescient about solving every difficulty; or the smart-mouthed Benson/Brighella, so

---

[4] I am indebted here to Thomas F. Heck's overview of *commedia* performance elements (1988).

appealing that he inspired his own spin-off series. *Cheers* is another good resource; Woody/Arlecchino is both dumb and ingenuous; Frazer Crane/Dottore is so smart he's stupid and is much inclined to tirades of multi-syllabic verbosity. The only limitation to this classroom gambit is commonality: not everyone will recognize every example. But the enthusiasm that develops during an argument over whether or not Sam on *Cheers* is a lover or a braggart soldier can also animate a discussion of how Falstaff differs from the *miles gloriosus*. Students who remember the history of a character's development in a long-running series—say Margaret Hoolihan's transformation from bimbo to proto-feminist—can learn something about how comic types alter over time: the one dimensional "flat" character simply does not sustain interest over a ten-year span. Shakespeare's characters, too, became increasingly complex as his career developed. Once students see that knowing a character type well can allow them to predict how that character will behave in any given situation, they will understand more about how *commedia* improvisation worked. They may be able to do it themselves. Given a brief plot sketch and a character list, they may even be able to predict the action of a Shakespearean comedy before they have read it. Students can then read to find a pattern they already know, read to discover if the script defies or satisfies expectations. And their reading will be easier because of it: educated people always read with a paradigm, a context, in mind.

Such pedagogical mixing of what some might call low- and high-brow genres is not, I think, a problem. Shakespeare is certainly none the worse for it: connecting his popular drama with our own only makes his look that much better and reasserts Jonson's praise that "He was not of an age, but for all time!" More importantly, contemporary Pantalones make Shakespearean drama more comprehensible. Most important of all, recognizing that they *do* know a lot about a theatrical tradition that continues to entertain gives students the confidence to seek actively to know more, to read with understanding. American popular culture is an image-dominated culture (Paglia 1991, 181), and our students are quite adept at identifying those images; their skill can be put to good use in their service. E. M. Forster was pedagogically correct in his epigraph to *Howard's End:* "only connect." *Howard's End,* by the way, was released as a film in 1992. With any luck, some students will see it and then want to read it.

Works Cited

Heck, Thomas F. *Commedia dell'Arte: A Guide to the Primary and Secondary Literature.* New York: Garland, 1988.

Herrick, Marvin T. *Italian Comedy in the Renaissance.* Urbana: University of Illinois Press, 1960.

Horowitz, Joy. "Hollywood Law: Whose Idea Is It, Anyway?" *New York Times,* March 15, 1992, 2:1,23.

Lea, K. M. *Italian Popular Comedy.* 2 vols. 1934. Reprint. New York: Russell & Russell, 1962.

McWilliam, G. H. *Shakespeare's Italy Revisited.* Leicester: Leicester University Press, 1974.

Mellamphy, Ninian. "Pantaloons and Zanies: Shakespeare's 'Apprenticeship' to Italian Professional Comedy Troupes." In *Shakespearean Comedy,* edited by Maurice Charney, 141–51. New York: New York Literary Forum, 1980.

Paglia, Camille. "Junk Bonds and Corporate Raiders: Academe in the Hour of the Wolf." *Arion* 1:2 (Spring 1991): 139–212.

Singal, Daniel J. "The Other Crisis in American Education." *Atlantic Monthly* (November 1991): 61–65.

Teague, Frances. "*Othello* and New Comedy." *Comparative Drama* 20:1 (1986): 54–64.

Zancha, Richard B. "Iago and the *Commedia dell'Arte.*" *Arlington Quarterly* 2:2 (1969): 98–116.

Contributors

Paul C. Castagno is an Assistant Professor of Theatre and Director of the New Playwrights' Program at the University of Alabama.

Nancy L. D'Antuono is Assistant Professor of Italian at Saint Mary's College, Notre Dame, Indiana. She is the author of a book on the Italian *novella* and the theatre of Lope de Vega, as well as many articles on Italo-Hispanic literary relations as they pertain to the *commedia dell'Arte*, the *commedia erudita*, and Spanish Golden Age drama.

James Fisher is Associate Professor of Theatre at Wabash College, Crawfordsville, Indiana, and is the author of *The Theatre of Yesterday and Tomorrow:* Commedia dell'Arte *on the Modern Stage.*

Thomas F. Heck is Professor of Music History and Head of the Music/Dance Library at The Ohio State University. He is the author of Commedia dell'Arte: *A Guide to the Primary and Secondary Literature.*

Stanley V. Longman is Professor of Drama at the University of Georgia and Director of its Study Abroad Program in Parma, Italy, and London, England.

Jane McMahan is Associate in Music at Barnard College and a graduate student in theatre at the CUNY Graduate School.

Anna L. Moro is a Ph.D. candidate in Italian Linguistics at the University of Toronto.

Georgeann Murphy is Associate Professor of Dramatic Arts and English at Centre College in Danville, Kentucky.

Christopher C. Newton is a doctoral candidate in theatre at Tufts University.

Thomas A. Pallen is Associate Professor of Theatre at Austin Peay State University in Clarksville, Tennessee; he directs and designs for the Roxy Community Theatre, and spends summers in Cortona, Italy.

Michael L. Quinn is Assistant Professor in the School of Drama at the University of Washington in Seattle. He is the author of *The Semiotic Stage: Prague School Theater Theory* and several other articles and books on the theatre.

John Swan is the Head Librarian at Bennington College. He is the co-author, with Martin Green, of *The Triumph of Pierrot: The* Commedia dell'Arte *and the Modern Imagination*.